Teaching Tips for Challenging Behaviors

Practical Strategies to Help Teachers
Manage, Monitor, Document, and Improve School Success
for Students with and without Specific Disabilities

by
Debra Kitzman
and Kelly Gunzenhauser

illustrated by
Julie Anderson

Key Education Publishing
An imprint of Carson-Dellosa Publishing Company LLC
Greensboro, North Carolina

www.keyeducationpublishing.com

CONGRATULATIONS ON YOUR PURCHASE OF A KEY EDUCATION PRODUCT!

The editors at Key Education are former teachers who bring experience, enthusiasm, and quality to each and every product. Thousands of teachers have looked to the staff at Key Education for new and innovative resources to make their work more enjoyable and rewarding. We are committed to developing educational materials that will assist teachers in building a strong and developmentally appropriate curriculum for young children.

PLAN FOR GREAT TEACHING EXPERIENCES WHEN YOU USE EDUCATIONAL MATERIALS FROM KEY EDUCATION PUBLISHING

About the Authors

Debra Kitzman has 12 years experience teaching five year olds. She has a master's degree in Special Education from John's Hopkins University. Prior to having a family she taught Middle School in Maryland for four years then worked with Jr. High ESL students in Minnesota for two years. She enjoys reading and spending time on High Rock Lake in North Carolina with her husband and yellow lab, Sandy.

Kelly Gunzenhauser teaches two-year-olds. She has a master's degree in English and has been an editor and writer in the educational publishing field for over 13 years. She is an avid school volunteer. She lives in Winston-Salem with her husband and two active kids!

Credits
Authors: Debra Kitzman & Kelly Gunzenhauser
Project Director: Sherrill B. Flora
Illustrator: Julie Anderson
Editor: Claude Chalk
Cover Design & Production: Annette Hollister-Papp
Page Layout: Key Education Staff
Cover Photographs: © ShutterStock

Key Education
An imprint of Carson-Dellosa Publishing LLC
PO Box 35665
Greensboro, NC 27425 USA
www.keyeducationpublishing.com

ISBN 978-1-60268-116-3
02-028138091

Contents

Introduction

Does one of these situations sound familiar?

In your class of four-year-olds, you have a student with Down's Syndrome. She is a joy to have in class. However, she cannot hold a crayon, her speech is very hard to understand (even though she clearly likes to chat with other students), and her gross motor skills are very poor. You are happy to work with her on these things, but you need some fresh ideas for how to help her make some progress.

In late September, a new student enrolled in your readiness class. His parents were told that their son was not ready for public school, and they were asked to take him out after repeated visits to the principal's office. Already, you find yourself saying his name constantly. He willfully breaks toys, and either ignores directions or says, "I won't do it!" The student is brimming with anger and often takes it out on you and his classmates. You are at the end of your rope, and so is the student's family.

In your first-grade classroom of 25 students, you find yourself spending a huge amount of time with one of the younger ones. He is clearly bright enough to handle the work, but he cannot sit still for five minutes before he is up and out of his seat, or talking to another student, or even rolling around on the floor. How can you manage this student's behavior while still giving your other students the attention and time they deserve?

Some students need extra help right from the beginning.

If you are a teacher, something similar to at least one of these scenarios has probably popped up during your career. Teachers can often see how certain challenging behaviors and developmental deficits will continue to limit students' achievement for the rest of their academic careers and beyond. It is up to teachers and parents to work together to assist these students who have behavioral or developmental challenges to overcome. The goal for the student with Down's Syndrome is to learn to communicate clearly so that she can complete her education and one day, hopefully, get a job. The student in the readiness class must learn self-control and how to get along with others if he hopes to make friends and enjoy school. The student who cannot sit still must learn to stay on task or he will be unable to complete projects and study for tests.

As a teacher, you already know that some behaviors and developmental issues are likely to frustrate students now and create even greater problems down the line. *Teaching Tips for Young Kids with Challenging Behaviors* is for those students and the teachers who teach them. This book examines many of the behavioral and developmental issues teachers of young students come across, and offers simple but creative ideas for giving these students the extra help they may need.

Are all of the behaviors in this book a result of developmental disabilities?

Many (but not all) of the behaviors in this book can potentially be attributed to physical and developmental disabilities, but this book does not attempt to diagnose specific disabilities. For one thing, teachers offer valuable insight into student behaviors, but only trained specialists should actually diagnose disabilities. Second, many disabilities are very difficult to diagnose before early elementary age, because preschoolers are still developing. For example, a student who is too young to learn to read cannot show obvious signs that she is dyslexic. For these reasons, this book focuses on behaviors, and not on what underlying problems may be causing them.

What will I find in this book?

Each chapter names an over-arching behavior or developmental area, such as Physical Development or Language and Literacy. In each chapter, you will find a list of subsections, like fine and gross motor skills, or clarity of speech and language acquisition. Each of these sections lists signs of failure to develop in this area, and provides helpful and simple suggestions for helping students catch up with classmates, unlearn the behavior, or otherwise improve. Finally, each chapter includes two activity sheets related to identifying problem areas, helping students to improve, and/or tracking progress.

Additionally, there are several teacher worksheets that can help you assess and observe, track student progress, plan the school day, and communicate with parents. These pages will help you keep your documentation organized, and will let you see at a glance where a student has been and where he is going.

Chapter 1
Using the Observation Form, Action Record, Planning Page, and Communication Forms

Observation Form

Use the Observation Form (page 6) to record anything significant you notice about a student. You may be looking for specific issues as you do observations. However, if you frequently make observations about a student, even if you are not sure what you are looking for, patterns may emerge. There are several different types of observations.

- ❖ **Silent Observations** involve watching the student work and interact in the classroom, either alone or with other students and teachers. You are not an active part of the observation.

- ❖ **Interactive Observations** happen when you are talking, working, or playing with the student. You record both your actions and words and the students'.

- ❖ **"Paperwork Observations"** include notes about anything you observe on student work. These observations could be about anything from artwork subject matter selection, to letter formation, to a test score.

- ❖ **Family Observations** will be more unusual, but can be very helpful. For example, if you use this form to document behavior that could possibly result from abuse, you can record how the student acts around each parent and then compare your notes as you prepare your report.

- ❖ If you want to include observations from multiple days on one form, simply add additional dates to the Observation Notes and Follow-Up sections.

Action Record (page 7)

Once you target a challenging behavior or skill deficit, you may want to track different strategies you try with the student, and whether or not they are successful. This page has space for you to list several different strategies and their results.

Weekly Planning Form (page 8)

Every teacher needs a good planning form. This form can be used alone or in conjunction with the Action Record (page 7) as you work on helping a student. Simply fill in either theme and centers (preschool) or special events and subject areas (elementary school), then plan your strategies for helping students. For example, if you are helping a student who has trouble hearing, you can make a note to seat him next to the speakers during a computer presentation.

Communication Forms (page 9)

Students who need extra help do not just need *your* help. Family help and support are extremely important, as well. Partner with parents by sending home short progress reports. For a parent who is concerned about his child, a short note is both an update and a reminder that you are on the job.

Observation Form

Student's Name: _____ Date of Observation: _____

Student's Date of Birth: _____ Time of Observation: _____

Purpose of Observation: _____

Place of Observation: _____

Observation Notes:

Follow-Up:

Teacher Signature: _____

Action Record Form

Student's Name: _____ Student's Date of Birth: _____

Purpose for This Action Record: _____

_____

Date: _____ Action and Results:

Date: _____ Action and Results:

Date: _____ Action and Results:

Planning Form for Week of _____

Themes or Special Events: _____

	Monday	Tuesday	Wednesday	Thursday	Friday
Centers or Subject Areas					

Please see me!

Date: _____

Dear Parent or Guardian,

I would like to talk with you about _____.
Let's set up a time for a conference/phone call. Can we talk on
_____? Thank you!

Sincerely,

_____

Good Effort Today by _____! Date: _____

_____

_____

_____

Sincerely, _____

Date: _____   _____ # Needs to Work On...

_____

_____

_____

Sincerely, _____

Here's an observation about _____: Date: _____

_____

_____

_____

Sincerely, _____

❖ **poor fine motor skills** ❖ **poor gross motor skills** ❖
❖ **lack of spatial awareness or difficulty with directionality** ❖
❖ **poor eyesight** ❖ **poor hearing** ❖ **other physical disabilities** ❖

In a typical preschool classroom, students' physical development may vary widely and still be "normal." Josh may prefer to play with blocks and cars, but show little interest in catching balls, while Cara would rather run and climb on the playground equipment than try to draw or cut. But especially in preschool, teachers must find innovative ways to support **balanced growth** in fine and gross motor skills. The key is to make students comfortable with both areas so that avoidance does not turn into outright resistance.

Elementary students are expected to be proficient at fine and gross motor skills—ready to pick up a pencil and trace letters, and also to handle the playground equipment with ease. Undoubtedly, fine motor skills are often more valued in elementary school because of the amount of writing that is expected, but students benefit from having confidence in their gross motor abilities, and physical exercise is crucial to students' health.

Many classrooms contain students with diagnosed physical challenges that affect their hearing, sight, spatial awareness, directionality, gross motor skills, and/or fine motor skills. In these cases, if the physical challenge is serious enough, you will be well aware of the situation, and parents will usually request a conference about how their child can be successful in the classroom. However, there will be some students whose physical challenges are subtle, or even undiscovered. For example, a student with poor vision may be undiagnosed because she has learned to cope with it in most situations by squinting, sitting close to the board, or looking at a friend's paper. Whether a student has a diagnosis or not, it is important to make accommodations and implement creative strategies, such as the ones in this chapter, that will help the student succeed in your classroom.

Poor Fine Motor Skills

It is not uncommon for some students to struggle with fine motor skills. Especially in preschool, some students seem naturally to prefer fine motor activities to gross motor activities (or vice-versa), and this is perfectly normal. But, avoiding fine motor tasks can lead to difficulty with writing letters and numbers, therefore undermining reading and math skills. In most cases, fine motor skills significantly improve between ages three and four. A majority of five- and six-year-olds should be able to fasten most pieces of clothing and draw recognizable shapes, letters, and numbers. In cases where students seem behind their peers in fine motor skills, it is important to use activities that build fine-motor confidence and help get students ready to write.

Indicators of Poor Fine Motor Skills

❖ Has a poor crayon or pencil grip. (May grip with fist, or have trouble with pincer grip.)
❖ Has difficulty coloring within lines. (Coloring is more like scribbling.)
❖ Dislikes writing and art activities.
❖ Uses eating utensils awkwardly. (Grabs utensils with a fist, frequently loses food off of utensils, or shuns utensils altogether.)
❖ Eats sloppily (Food does not make it into the mouth easily.)
❖ Shows poor hand-eye coordination.
❖ Dislikes playing with toys that have small pieces, such as blocks, marbles, and board games.
❖ Avoids computer mouse and keyboard; lacks interest in exploring age-appropriate electronic games.
❖ Has difficulty using scissors. (Cannot open or close scissors or cut along lines; holds them upside down.)
❖ Does messy written work. (Coloring and letter and number formation are sloppy compared to peers.)

Tricks and Tips for Improving Fine Motor Skills

❖ **Provide fine motor tools on the playground** to entice students who prefer gross motor activities: sidewalk chalk, string for weaving around a chain-link fence, small sand tools, and toy cars for racing down the slide.

❖ **Purchase pencil grippers** that slide over pencils and create a proper pincer grip.

❖ **Use primary pencils** with a larger circumference.

❖ **Let the student mold a piece of modeling clay around her pencil.** The clay will help her grip the pencil, and playing with the modeling clay will strengthen hand muscles.

❖ **Let students write with tiny sample crayons** or golf pencils to create the proper pincer grip.

❖ **Coloring is excellent fine motor practice.** Use white glue to draw an outline of a simple drawing. When the glue dries, it will form a raised border that will help the student color within the boundary more easily.

❖ **Try using markers, colored pencils, or larger crayons.** Crayons are often dull and hard to manage because they break when held firmly. If students are frustrated with crayons, try markers, colored pencils, or larger crayons.

❖ **Write each student's name in highlighter, or print each student's name on the computer.** Let students use pencils to trace their names. For older students, print their names on handwriting lines, or write them with a black marker. Let students place blank paper over the writing and trace the black lines that show through.

❖ **Let students set a classroom table with plastic utensils, paper plates, and napkins.** Provide chunks of fruit or cheese. Sit with a few students each day and practice holding utensils properly.

❖ **Always have each student clean up under her own eating area using a small hand broom and dustpan.** Cleaning the floor or table makes students aware of whether they are eating neatly. Coordinating the broom and dustpan is excellent fine motor and hand-eye coordination practice.

- **Provide plenty of small manipulatives for students ages four and up.** Use expected ones (Legos, lacing cards, puzzles, number cubes) as well as unusual ones, like dominos for setting up domino runs, coins to put into a piggy bank, gloves, and brushes and combs for styling doll hair. Older students can play fine-motor games like Bingo, Trouble, Battleship, Bananagrams, and Connect Four.

- **Let young students trace inside of plastic switch plate covers and letter stencils, or trace around coins.** Use the Shape Stencils (page 13) to give students practice with different shapes. (Note: You can use this technique to make themed stencil laminates for holidays and other units. Copy a recognizable holiday shape, laminate it, and cut out the picture, leaving the remaining paper in tact. Use the resulting cutout shapes as felt board manipulatives.)

- **Create a fine motor "toolbox" using a plastic tool box from a home improvement store.** Fill it with squishy balls, locks and keys, eyedroppers, chenille craft sticks, belts with buckles, strips of hook-and-loop tape, paperclip chains, and zippers. Let students use the toolbox at a center or during indoor recess.

- **Play music or a book on tape during manipulative time.** The added stimulation may help students settle down to work with them for a longer period of time.

- **If you have access to a computer, let reluctant students work with partners** who are eager to use the computer. Let the reluctant student watch until she expresses an interest in trying it herself.

- **Provide old typewriters or computer keyboards** as part of a center or during manipulative time. When students get to play with them, they will feel more comfortable in front of an actual computer.

- **Pinching clothespins increases strength in small hands.** Let students use clothespins to hang clothing in the housekeeping center, or to hang artwork on a child-height clothesline.

- **Have older students assemble bulletin boards.** Cutting paper and pushing in pushpins are excellent fine motor practice, and helping the teacher is its own reward.

- **Cut more than just paper.** Let students cut cardboard, straws, string, yarn, and magazine pages. Let them roll play dough into strings or push it through a string mold, press it onto a plastic doll's head, and cut "hair."

- **Motivate students to use scissors by asking for help with sending home reminder notes.** Compose the note, then put duplicate several copies on each sheet of paper. Ask a student to cut apart the notes with child-safe pinking shears or patterned scissors. (Be sure to supervise students around these sharper edges.)

- **Give the "gift" of fine motor skills.** Let students cut wrapping paper, apply tape, and use ruler edges to curl ribbon. If students wrap in pairs, one partner can hold down paper or ribbon while the other tapes or ties.

- **Incorporate artwork into fine motor practice.** Let students make collages by tearing and gluing torn paper into pictures. Other small items like dried pasta or popcorn kernels make great collage artwork, too.

- **Let students use watered-down paint and eyedroppers** to make raindrop pictures.

- **If you have students who love cars or trains,** let them assemble and play with sections of track.

- **Have a zipper / belt / shoelace / barrette / ponytail holder day.** Ask parents to send students to school wearing at least one of these items. Help a few students at a time master fastening their own items.

- **Mazes are excellent fine motor practice.** Use the School Bus Maze (page 14) to give students more practice with drawing continuous lines. For younger students, use a highlighter to trace the path from start to finish, and let students trace over it in pencil.

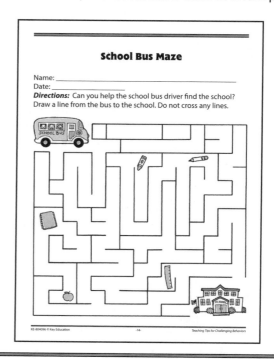

Shape Stencil

Copy the page onto card stock. Cut the card stock apart along the dashed lines. Laminate the shape cards. Use a craft knife to cut out each shape, leaving the paper outside the cut line intact, to make a stencil. Let students trace the shapes onto other sheets of paper. (Having students tape the cutouts to other pieces of paper offers even more fine motor practice.)

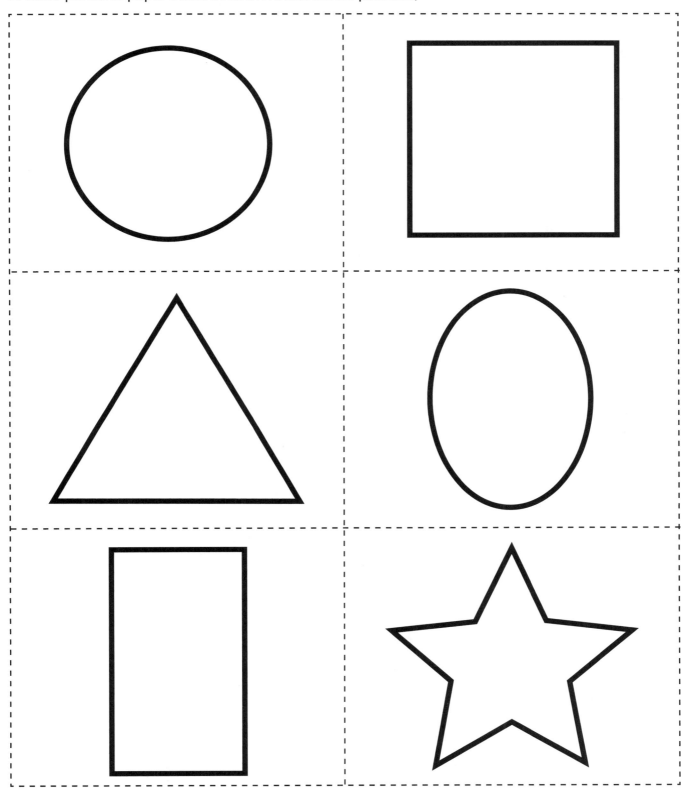

School Bus Maze

Name: _____

Date: _____

Directions: Can you help the school bus driver find the school? Draw a line from the bus to the school. Do not cross any lines.

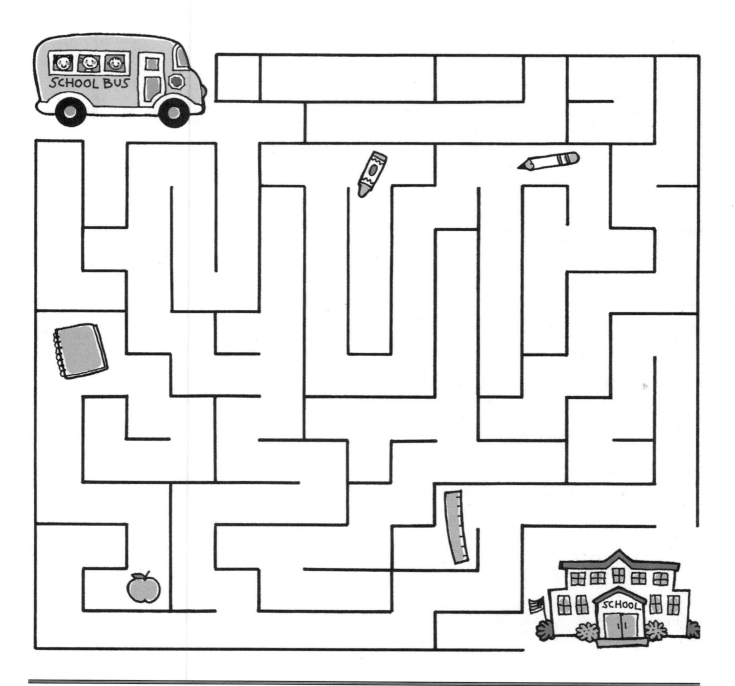

Poor Gross Motor Skills

Like fine motor skills, gross motor skills can be hard to gauge accurately in very young children, because there is such a large range of normal development. Unlike fine motor skills, good gross motor skills are rarely a part of daily classroom learning past preschool; gross motor activities are usually limited to general playground time and a once-a-week session with a physical education teacher. However, gross motor skills are important. Good gross motor skills help students develop general confidence and a well-rounded range of abilities. They give students who struggle academically another potential area in which to excel. And, with childhood obesity rates soaring, gross motor skill activities and physical education are experiencing a revival, and it is a good thing for students to be able to keep up.

Indicators of Poor Gross Motor Skills
- ❖ **Falls down excessively.**
- ❖ **Trips over own feet or objects.**
- ❖ **Walks on tiptoes.**
- ❖ **Uses two feet rather than alternating feet on stairs (after about age five).**
- ❖ **Falls out of chair.**
- ❖ **Bumps into others.**
- ❖ **Makes jerky movements.**
- ❖ **Has a strange gait when walking or running. (May flap arms, kick up heels too far, run with stiff legs, take giant steps or tiny steps, use "penguin walking," or arms and legs may be out of sync)**

Tricks and Tips for Improving Gross Motor Skills

- ❖ **If a student falls or bangs into objects often, recommend an eye check.** If no vision problems are present, then recommend a hearing test. Vision and sometimes hearing problems often contribute to poor balance and other gross motor deficits. Improving gross motor skills can be as simple as getting a new pair of glasses.

- ❖ **If young students are within developmentally appropriate ranges, gross motor skills should not be a concern.** Refer to the Gross Motor Chart (page 18) for a list of age-appropriate gross motor skill development.

- ❖ **Watch for students who stick close to the sand box during outside play.** They may be indicating that they are not comfortable with gross motor activities. Try to entice them into gross motor play.

- ❖ **When you toss something at a young student, her instinct may be to duck** rather than move into harm's way to catch the object. Overcome fears by starting slowly with throwing and catching. Instead of throwing balls, have students sit in a circle and roll balls to each other to learn how to grab for a ball without risk.

- ❖ **Large-scale body motions** (stretches, jumping jacks, running, doing crunches, bringing knees to chest, or squatting), will teach students' muscles how to work together. Add a few stretches, yoga moves, or gentle calisthenics into your daily routine to "get the wiggles out," build muscle memory, and ease transitions.

- ❖ **Balance beams are great for building core strength.** Have students walk on a low, raised beam or on a strip of colored tape.

- ❖ **When weather keeps you indoors, have a dance party!** Marching helps students develop coordination and balance as they alternate feet. Soft music encourages graceful movements, while energetic music inspires rapid movements. Try a combination of music to see what students enjoy.

- ❖ **Use music to encourage gross motor skills** in dramatic play, story time, and circle time. Let students act out songs about stomping dinosaurs, bouncing monkeys, flying bumblebees, and other animal actions.

- **Combine gross motor skills with other learning practice.** Laminate colored dots, shapes, letters, or numbers. Attach them to the floor with packing tape. Cover the sides of two dice with matching paper pieces. Call out a body part like, "Left hand," or "Right foot." Let a student roll the dice and place the corresponding body part on that shape. Continue playing, letting students place their hands and feet on the shapes they roll.

- **Is it cold outside?** Have each student squeeze a squishy ball between her knees and walk like a penguin.

- **Swinging a pole to hit a target** is easier if that target is fairly stationery, so celebrate birthdays with piñatas.

- **Stuck inside? Break the "walking feet" rule** and hold relay races in the hall, the gym, or the breezeway.

- **Find new treasures on the playground.** Once each month, use tape or sticky-tack to attach holiday gel clings, plastic eggs, plastic gems, chocolate coins (if it isn't hot), or plastic coins to the playground equipment. Make the objects match the theme of whatever holiday is coming up. Challenge students to climb all of the equipment to find the treasures.

- **Plastic hoops are a great gross motor tool.** Scatter them and have students run, crawl, wiggle, or leap frog from one to the next. Also, teach students to hula hoop using weighted hoops, which are much easier to use than lightweight hoops.

- **Use plastic hoops for target practice.** Students can toss rolled socks or beanbags through the hoops. This is an excellent upper body activity that helps students gauge how much strength they need to reach a distance.

- **Use plastic hoops, cones, rope, playground equipment, and other objects to create an obstacle course** that combines different gross motor skills into one challenge. (Have students put the hoops over their heads and drop them to the ground as part of the course.) Most students will excel in clearing at least one obstacle.

- **Do not let the playground get boring.** Introduce new games, and practice until students learn to play them. Read the Back to Basics: Old School Games list (page 19) for ideas.

- **Instead of pushing them all the time, help students learn to pump their legs on swings.** Swinging teaches balance and motion, as well as awareness of the distance to the ground, and of body position within the arc.

- **Some students walk on tiptoes.** They usually grow out of it, but at age four or five, this is an issue. Demonstrate and practice heel-toe walking. Roll out a large strip of white butcher paper. Paint a red splotch on the bottom of the student's heel, and a blue splotch under his toes. Have him walk red/blue red/blue.

- **To stretch out the Achilles tendons of students who have trouble walking heel–toe**, have them balance their toes on a low board, and try to lower their ankles to the floor.

- **Students who fall a lot may simply need to slow down.** When walking down the hall, play slow music and practice walking slowly. Have the an assistant or a classmate stand with at the back of the line and hold that student's hand to slow him down, or let him lead the line and walk with you.

- **If a student has trouble walking in a straight line,** have her gently run her hand along the wall as she walks down the hallway. (Let the whole class touch the wall, since they will probably do it anyway.)

- ❖ **People are "wired" to follow their eyes.** Students who look up or to the side when walking lose their balance because they cannot see where they are going. Saying, "Eyes front!" helps students avoid collisions by looking at the heads of the classmates ahead of them.

- ❖ **Depending on their size, students ages four and up should navigate stairs using alternating feet.** Hold the student's hand and let him hold the railing with his other hand as he practices walking on alternate feet up and down the steps. Show parents how to practice this skill at home with their children.

- ❖ **Some students, especially those with glasses, have poor depth perception** that can make stairs look more like ramps. Place a strip of colored tape on the top edge of each step to show students where each step ends.

- ❖ **The trick to improving students' gross motor skills is to keep them engaged in an activity** until their minds and bodies learn to work well and enjoyably together. It is important to try different activities at a young age. As students get older, developing these skills gets harder and self-consciousness becomes a factor. Encourage parents to introduce students to new activities like swimming, hiking, or skating that encourage vastly different gross motor skills. If a student can find one activity she enjoys, she may have confidence to try other things, and may develop muscles and coordination that create success in another area. For example, a student who loves to swim with a kick board may turn into a faster runner with stronger leg muscles.

Gross Motor Skill Guidelines

Use this as a rough guideline for what students should be able to do at different ages.

By age 2, most students can:

- ❑ Run and jump
- ❑ Walk on tiptoes
- ❑ Kick a ball
- ❑ Throw a ball
- ❑ Rock on a rocking horse

By age 3, most students can:

- ❑ Balance briefly on one foot
- ❑ Walk backwards
- ❑ Gallop
- ❑ Throw objects overhand with some accuracy
- ❑ "Catch" a rolled ball
- ❑ Pedal and steer a tricycle

By age 4, most students can:

- ❑ Hop on one foot more than one time
- ❑ Catch a large, tossed ball
- ❑ Bounce and catch a large ball
- ❑ Navigate stairs on alternating feet

By age 5, most students can:

- ❑ Alternate feet to skip
- ❑ Walk heel-toe
- ❑ Carry objects up and down stairs
- ❑ Walk on a balance beam
- ❑ Ride a bike with training wheels

By age 6, most students can:

- ❑ Jump over objects
- ❑ Throw with accuracy
- ❑ Dribble a basketball

(From this point, most students are capable of achieving most gross motor activities.)

Back to Basics: Old School Games

Encourage gross motor development with active games on the playground. Choose games according to what most of your students will be able to do. The more they practice, the better their muscle memory will be. Many of these games are fun inside, too.

Ring Around the Rosy/London Bridge: These activities combine music and movement. Young preschoolers will enjoy the songs, and the ideas of, "All fall down," and "Lock her up."

Mother May I: Have students line up on a starting line. Instruct them to take different types and numbers of steps, such as, "Take three giant steps," or "Take two tiny steps." Before stepping, students must ask, "Mother, may I?" Anyone who forgets to ask before moving must return to the starting line and begin again.

Duck, Duck, Goose: Have students sit in a circle. Let one student walk around the outside of the circle and gently tap classmates as he says, "Duck, Duck, etc. " When he says, "Goose," the tapped classmate must jump up and chase the student around the circle in order to tag him before he sits down. If the student is tagged, he sits in the center of the circle for the next round, and the classmate who tagged him takes a turn walking around the circle. If the running student is not tagged, the classmate sits in the center as the student takes another turn.

Hot Potato: Let students stand or sit in a circle and pass a soft ball around as you play upbeat music. When you stop the music, the student holding the ball is out. Continue until you have one student left.

Freeze Tag: Encourage students to chase and tag each other. If one student, "It," manages to tag and freeze all students before a student who is still running can tag and unfreeze anyone, then "It," gets to choose a new "It."

Red Light, Green Light: Line up students at a starting line and say, "Green light!" They should run toward a finish line until you say, "Red light!" They should all freeze. Any students who move must return to the starting line. The game ends when someone reaches the finish line.

The Limbo and Conga: Play Caribbean music and start a game of Limbo or a playground Conga line. The Limbo (bending backwards under an increasingly lower broomstick) encourages flexibility while the Conga (a dance in which students hold each other's waists while following a leader) improves coordination as students move forward, hopefully without stepping on each other.

Monkey in the Middle: Elementary students may enjoy a little competition, so let two students stand about 10 feet apart while a few classmates are the "monkeys" standing between them. The two students on the outside have to toss a ball back and forth without it being intercepted. If a student in the middle gets the ball, the student who threw it must take her place in the middle as one of the "monkeys." The student who caught the ball moves to the outside.

Jump the River: In a wide-open, grassy area, stretch two jump ropes so that they are parallel and just a couple of inches apart. Instruct students to line up and jump over them. When everyone has had a turn, move the ropes farther apart. As students step on the rope, they are out. The last student to clear the ropes is the winner.

Jump Rope: Do not forget to use jump ropes as they are meant to be used. Especially in elementary school, students will enjoy turning the rope for each other and jumping to different chants and rhymes.

Kickball: A great alternative to baseball, kickball uses the same rules and players, but students are kicking a soft, rubber ball instead of hitting a hard ball with a bat.

Lack of Spatial Awareness, or Difficulty with Directionality

This student is easy to spot; he is constantly knocking things over, bumping into friends, and clipping the wall when he turns a corner. Spatial unawareness is common in young children because they grow so fast and are not aware of the new size of their limbs. Often, these students have good gross motor skills in that they can throw a ball far or run fast, but they have not learned their own strength, or how to gauge distances from themselves to objects. When you have outside playtime, these students are most likely to be injured, mostly from accidents that happen when their exuberance exceeds their awareness of objects in their paths.

Lack of spatial awareness can be caused by poor depth perception and lack of peripheral vision, as well as near- and farsightedness. Poor vision limits a student's ability to gauge distances, which often creates difficulties when doing simple things like moving and walking. But, students certainly can have a lack of spatial awareness even when they have perfect vision. Even the student with the best eyesight can wreak havoc when he runs looking over his shoulder.

Students with poor directionality are those who cannot find their way to the cafeteria after weeks of school, who hold up their left hands when you say, "Raise your right hands," who have trouble backtracking without reversed directions, and who cannot mimic your actions or memorize movements easily. (The Hokey Pokey can be a true challenge.) The following activities can help both kinds of students learn to find their way without getting lost or injured.

Indicators of Lack of Spatial Awareness
* Does not see when objects are in the way. (Plowing through objects instead of walking around them)
* Has difficulty gauging distances.
* Bangs elbows and knees on things.
* Constantly finds sharp corners—ouch!
* Drifts to one side when walking.
* Seems disoriented when turning around.
* Stumbles when eyes are not facing front.
* Cannot clap or march to a beat.
* Falls down or out of chairs.
* Trips over own feet or objects.
* Falls up steps.
* Bumps into others.
* Is uncoordinated when running or has a strange gait (flapping arms, kicking up heels too far, stiff legs, feet too far apart, takes giant or tiny steps, arms and legs out of sync).
* Has difficulty catching a ball; ducks or shields head when a ball is thrown.

Indicators of Difficulty with Directionality
* Cannot easily tell right from left.
* Unable to follow directional commands, like "Turn right."
* Cannot easily copy others' motions.
* Has difficulty with directional patterning and retracing steps.

Tricks and Tips for Lack of Spatial Awareness and Difficulty with Directionality

❖ **Suggest that parents get the student's eyes checked,** including depth perception and peripheral vision.

❖ **If the student gets glasses, she may need time to adjust to differences in depth perception and peripheral vision,** so watch out for a few more accidents than usual, and expect timidity with outside activity.

❖ **Let students work with shape sorters** to improve their visual skills.

❖ **If students have a hard time walking down steps,** place a strip of colored tape on the end of each step. Use different colors of tape so that the student knows a separate step is under each color.

❖ **For students who tend to walk into walls,** have a classmate walk between the wall and the other student. Or, let the student run one hand along the wall while walking to maintain a consistent distance from the wall.

❖ **Remind young students, "Look down and around before you start moving!"** If you get them in the habit of looking down and around before they move, they may have fewer tripping accidents.

❖ **Tape paper shapes or plastic hoops on the floor.** Have students walk around the room and put each of their feet entirely inside each shape. Or, have them walk around and avoid putting their feet into the shapes.

❖ **Create a path on the floor, like a maze,** by lining up cereal boxes, blocks, cones, empty aluminum cans, or classroom chairs. Challenge students to walk through a different path each day without knocking over the objects.

❖ **Encourage students to "fist bump" and "high five" with friends.** It is amazing to see how difficult it can be for students to connect.

❖ **Magnetic fishing is a great spatial activity** because students have to see where the fish is to know where to cast the line. Cut out paper fish and attach a paper clip to each. Tie one end of a string to a stick, and the other end to a magnet, then let students cast the fishing line and try to attract fish.

❖ **Catching is hard for young students to master, but when older students are not able to judge the location** of a ball in the air, they need help training their eyes and hands to work together. Have them practice throwing and catching soft balls or textured balls until they get the hang of it. (Baseball mitts can help with catching.)

❖ **Tetherball is a great spatial exercise** for elementary students. Students do not actually have to catch the ball, and with practice, they will learn to judge the distance from themselves to the ball as it swings by them.

❖ **Let students make a game out of bouncing** off the walls. Have them hold out their hands and "bounce" from side to side in a hallway. Younger students can do this in a doorway.

❖ **Have each student place a hoop over the head of a classmate**, then lower the hoop to the floor without touching the classmate's body.

❖ **If you are doing calisthenics as a class,** or if you are teaching a dance for a program, do all motions with your back to students so they can follow the correct hands and feet.

❖ **Which way should I go?** When you get to the end of a hallway and you are going somewhere familiar to students, ask them to tell you which way to turn next.

❖ **Be consistent when moving as a class.** For example, always walk down the right side of the hallway. Stop at predictable places, and avoid sudden stops if you want to avoid a student pile-up.

❖ **If you run across any "magical eye" pictures,** purchase them for older students to play with. Trying to see the images help students work on their depth perception.

Tricks and Tips for Improving Directionality

❖ **The left hand trick.** Teach students who know their letters that the hand that makes the correct "L" with thumb and forefinger is the left hand.

❖ **Tape the letters L and R to students' sleeves** and shoes, to help them identify left and right body parts.

❖ **Tape left and right paper footprints to the floor.** Add left and right paper handprints to the wall. Label the cutouts with L and R or with the entire word if students are reading. Let students match their own hands and feet to the paper shapes.

Can You Get Through the Path?

Name: _____ Date: _____

Directions: Circle things the student might bump into.
Draw a line to lead the student to the door.

Which Box?

Name: _____ Date: _____

Directions: Draw a line from each shape to the picture that will fit inside of it.

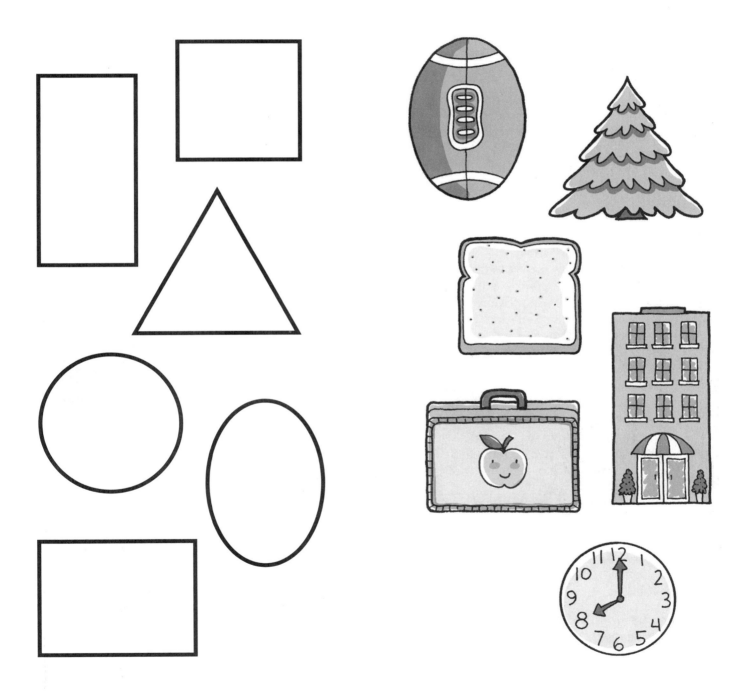

Poor Eyesight

It can be tough to figure out that a student has poor vision. Often it comes on so gradually that the student develops subtle ways of compensating for not being able to see. Very young students may have immature eye muscles that cause their eyes not to work well together, so they squint or cover one eye, and that behavior continues if vision starts to worsen. Vision problems can be a challenge to discover in older students, too, because of their coping skills. Unfortunately, untreated vision problems tend to get worse as students' eyes grow.

Vision problems can include simple nearsightedness or farsightedness, amblyopia (lazy eye) or strabismus (eyes not pointing in the same direction), lack of depth perception or peripheral vision, and even partial or total vision loss. Watch for the indicators below to help parents detect poor vision, then use the suggestions to make life easier for students who have to adjust to various vision problems.

Indicators of Poor Eyesight
- ❖ Squints, or closes/covers one eye.
- ❖ Rubs eyes.
- ❖ Has frequent headaches.
- ❖ Leans forward to try to see.
- ❖ Holds papers and books close. (This does not apply to children younger than four. They are still learning to make their eyes work together better and often pull reading materials close to their faces in concentration.)
- ❖ Does not recognize faces or motions from a distance.
- ❖ Is inattentive, especially during group reading time or movie time.
- ❖ Complains about needing more light.
- ❖ Cannot correctly copy shapes, letters, and numbers.
- ❖ Cannot copy from the board.
- ❖ Loses place when reading or copying.
- ❖ Fails to count or learn letters when looking at them on the board or a poster, but can do it easily from memory or close-up.
- ❖ Has difficulty telling when something is in the way. (Plows through objects.)
- ❖ Cannot gauge distances.
- ❖ Constantly falls down or runs into objects.
- ❖ Cannot catch a ball; ducks when a ball is thrown.
- ❖ Seems not to notice movement to the right or left.

Tricks and Tips for Dealing with Poor Eyesight

- ❖ **Be sure to visit the activities from the Lack of Spatial Awareness section (pages 22–23).** Although it is a separate issue, students who have poor vision may also have poor spatial awareness.

- ❖ **If you have a hunch that one of your students cannot see well, test all students with the Eye Chart (page 26).** While this chart will not be as accurate as a doctor's visit, it can help you decide if parents need to look into vision testing.

- ❖ **Routinely seat the student with poor vision in the front of the class or circle.** Not only does sitting closer help the student see better, it removes other objects and students from his field of vision, which can help him concentrate on seeing more easily.

- ❖ **Provide adequate light in your classroom.** If a student has very poor vision, consider asking parents to provide a battery powered clamp-on lamp or flashlight to help the student read.

- ❖ **Mix in large-print books** and images with your regular classroom materials.

- ❖ **When you read aloud often to students as a class** or in small groups, have students with poor vision sit close by to see the pictures. Allow good readers to partner with visually impaired students and read aloud to them.

- ❖ **There are many quality children's audio books available.** For students who are old enough to use the equipment themselves, set up a listening station with headphones and both print and audio copies of books. You can record yourself or parent volunteers reading the books, too, to expand your library inexpensively.

- ❖ **Use dark-colored markers when writing on the white board or chart paper.** Stick to blue, purple, or black; red is a favorite of teachers but is difficult to read.

- ❖ **If you post letter or number cutouts on a wall,** make sure the paper color contrasts with the wall color. Even if you use a color of paper that is different from the wall color, if the tone is similar, they will still be very hard to see. For example, if you have cream-colored walls, post shapes in dark blue or magenta, and stay away from white or pastel paper.

- ❖ **Contrasting colors.** If you have students trace shapes, letters, or numbers, provide traceable shapes in highly contrasting colors. Do not use light colors on white paper.

- ❖ **Do not hang double-sided posters or pictures over windows** or in front of a light source. Light coming in makes the image on the back shine through the image on the front. If you want to hang double-sided images, copy each side, then hang two copies, backing each image with opaque paper.

- ❖ **Keep letters simple and neat** when writing for children who have a hard time seeing.

- ❖ **Exaggerating the space between words helps students** concentrate on one written word at a time.

- ❖ **Make sure reproducibles are clear and sharp, with simple fonts.**

- ❖ **It is hard for some students to see dotted cut lines on worksheets.** Trace over reproducible cut lines with a marker to create larger cut lines that are easier to see from both sides of the scissors.

- ❖ **Assign helpers to assist with cutting, tracing,** or any fine motor skill that might be difficult for the student to see well enough to complete it on her own. The visually impaired student should still be able to do some of the work, but letting others help her will prevent her from getting frustrated and will give other students a chance to do something kind for a classmate. (And, it gives them more fine motor practice!)

- ❖ **Fine motor toys should be on a large scale for students who have visual impairments.** Provide puzzles with larger pieces, beads with larger holes, and geoboards with larger pegs.

- ❖ **Classmates can help a student with poor peripheral vision get around more easily.** Assign buddies to walk down the hall together.

- ❖ **Keep the room neat and the furniture arrangement consistent** so the visually impaired student has clear, recognizable paths to follow. If you do have to rearrange the classroom, take the student with poor vision on a guided tour when the classroom is otherwise empty to give him a chance to learn the new layout.

- ❖ **Avoid playground games like Red Rover** that have students running past each other, to avoid collisions.

- ❖ **If you have swings on the playground,** place a few large toys or cones in front of the swings to create a boundary that visually impaired students can easily see.

- ❖ **Getting glasses is a big deal,** so celebrate with a glasses party. Have students color and decorate the My New Glasses reproducible (page 27), cut out the glasses, and wear them the day a student walks in with new glasses.

Eye Chart

Use this eye chart to help you compare different students' vision. Post the chart on a wall. Have students stand twenty feet away and tell you the name of each shape, letter, or number. (Use only shapes for nonreaders.) This will not give you an exact reading but it can tell you which students might be having problems.

The distance and font size determine visual acuity.
Use this grid of font sizes to create your own accurate Snellen chart:

Distance (feet)	70	60	50	40	30	20	15	10	7	4
Letter height (mm)	31	27	22	18	13	9	7	4	3	2
Letter height (pt)	88	76	63	50	38	25	19	13	9	5
Font size (pt)	152	130	108	87	65	43	33	21	15	9

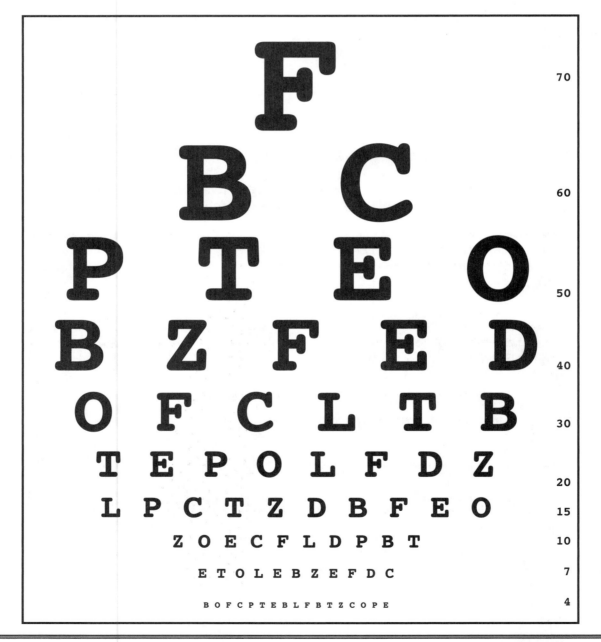

My New Glasses

Directions: Color the glasses. Cut them out and wear them!

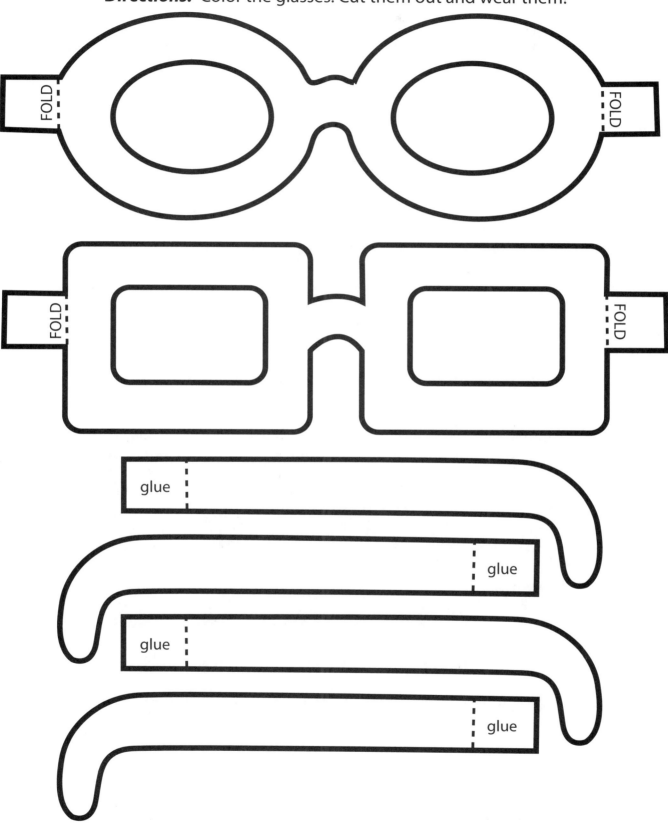

Poor Hearing

Like vision loss, hearing loss can be challenging to diagnose in young students. Since their language skills are just developing, and students are truly "all over the place" in terms of how quickly they learn to talk, how clear their speech is, and how fast their vocabularies expand, it can take a significant amount of time for even the most observant teacher to recommend a hearing test for a student.

To complicate matters, there are several different hearing difficulties. Hearing loss is the most familiar. Hyperacusis—hypersensitive hearing—is another type of hearing issue that makes regular noises louder than normal, and loud noises painful. Finally, there is auditory processing disorder. (For more information about these different hearing issues, refer to the Hearing Loss Guide on page 30.)

There are simple ways to put a student's hearing to a test just by calling his name or noticing his reactions to loud noises. Read below for a list of other possible indicators of hearing loss, and ideas for helping students who do have problems.

Indicators of Poor Hearing or Other Hearing Problems

❖ Says, "What?" or "Huh?" frequently.

❖ Cannot consistently repeat directions back to you. (If the student can repeat them consistently, he may be practicing "selective hearing" and not have true hearing loss.)

❖ Has difficulty following two-step directions. (This can be especially true for students with auditory processing disorder, since they sometimes transpose words that they hear.)

❖ It is necessary to touch the student when you speak to her in order to get her to pay attention.

❖ Cannot hear you unless you speak directly to his face.

❖ It is necessary to speak loudly on a regular basis. The student may also speak loudly as if she has trouble hearing herself.

❖ Does not react to loud stimuli, such as a fire alarm, a passing fire engine or airplane flying over.

❖ Complains about not being able to hear computer, TV, or headphones. Turns up the volume excessively.

❖ Has trouble hearing conversation over background noises. Cannot filter out extraneous noise.

❖ Shows confusion or has no reaction when others mumble or speak softly.

❖ May not respond to music like other students

❖ Has trouble sounding out a pitch; or cannot "find" a note. (Does not only affect students with poor hearing.)

❖ Speech may be unclear.

❖ Vocabulary lags behind other students or norms for the student's age group.

❖ Has trouble with letter-sound recognition (phonemic and phonetic problems).

❖ Has difficulty imitating sounds or words that other children like to repeat, like nursery rhymes or songs. (Students with auditory processing disorder may say the correct words, but not in the correct order.)

❖ In cases of hyperacusis (oversensitive hearing), covers hands at both loud noises and at noises that do not bother other students.

❖ Students who use headphones after the student with hyperacusis may complain that the sound is too low.

❖ Students with auditory processing disorder may hear words but have trouble putting them together to make meaning.

Tricks and Tips for Dealing with Poor Hearing

❖ **To test whether students have "selective hearing" or true hearing loss,** ask them to repeat directions back to you. If they can repeat the directions correctly, they may just be choosing not to follow them. Students with know hearing loss or with auditory processing disorder will benefit from repeating directions regularly.

❖ **Make sure students are quiet** before you address them with important instructions.

❖ **For older students, supplement verbal directions with a written version.** Give students simple instructions written on a card. As you talk to the rest of the class, students with cards can follow along as you speak.

❖ **Do not talk to the wall or the board, or cover your hand with your mouth when you speak.** Face students so they can see your lips move as you speak.

❖ **Do not talk while eating or chewing gum**, and do not mumble.

❖ **Do not talk while other "things" are talking.** Pause videos or music before you speak.

❖ **Instruct classmates to follow your lead by speaking clearly, making eye contact when speaking,** and avoiding turning their faces away when speaking to the student who is hearing impaired.

❖ **Model respectful behavior toward a student with hearing loss.** Maintain a calm, clear voice when speaking to her. If you must raise your voice when talking to her, do not add an "angry" tone. Doing so will lead classmates to believe you are angry or impatient with her for not being able to hear you. Classmates may adopt these same habits, so be sure to set a good example.

❖ **Seat a hearing impaired student close to the front of the room, or near where you give directions.**

❖ **You may need to address the obvious.** If the student already has a hearing impairment and wears hearing aids, make sure parents send the hearing aids to school. If a student stops paying attention, ask parents to check the hearing aid batteries.

❖ **Earwax buildup and ear infections can easily cause hearing loss.** Ask parents to have their child's ears checked for wax or infection before referring them to a hearing specialist.

❖ **Decide what is a reasonable volume for videos.** You want the student with hearing loss to be able to hear but not at the expense of classmates. You may have to strike a bargain with classmates to be exceptionally quiet in order for that student to hear at a reasonable volume, or allow the student with a hearing impairment to use headphones or follow closed captioning, if he can read.

❖ **Headphones are also a good idea for students with auditory processing disorder.** Even if they are not turned on, these students can concentrate better on what they are doing without extraneous noise.

❖ **Remember that established classroom routines and rules of favorite games are familiar territory for the hearing impaired student.** Sticking to familiar routines and rules will help the hearing impaired student proceed with confidence. If you do change rules or routines, review the changes ahead of time with the hearing impaired student so that you are not trying to explain the rules to two audiences (hearing impaired and non-hearing impaired) at the same time. The hearing impaired student will benefit from hearing them alone and then with the group.

❖ **If the hearing impaired student has a shadow who interprets or signs,** introduce the shadow to classmates, and explain in a matter-of-fact manner why she is there and what her job is. Let classmates ask questions and get to know her as another member of the classroom.

❖ **If possible, spend time as a whole class learning some sign language.** Students will enjoy finger spelling, and the hearing impaired student will appreciate the effort they make to communicate with him. Use the Sign Language Alphabet (page 31) to teach the alphabet and a few important words.

Hearing Loss Guide

Congenital Hearing Loss: Congenital hearing loss is present from birth. It can be caused by certain infections during pregnancy, ingestion of toxic medicines, complications during delivery, a disorder of the brain or nervous system, genetic syndromes, or simply by heredity. Hearing loss may be total or partial. Some types of hearing loss are correctable, either through surgery or hearing aids.

Acquired Hearing Loss: Acquired hearing loss happens after birth. Middle-ear infections, other infections or diseases, damage to eardrums, loud noises, head injury, some medications, and even earwax build-up can cause temporary or permanent damage to children's hearing. Sometimes, hearing loss can be corrected. Having earwax removed, or inserting tubes into the eardrum to allow the middle ear to drain and prevent infections, can immediately improve a child's hearing.

Tinnitus: Tinnitus is an internal ringing or buzzing noise. The noise may be intermittent or constant. It is as common in children as it is in adults. It can be caused by certain medications, injury to the ear or jaw, loud noises, and even occasionally tumors. Children often adapt to the noise, and frequently grow out of it.

Hyperacusis: Hyperacusis means oversensitive hearing. In cases of hyperacusis, the brain interprets sounds differently. Regular noises are perceived as too loud, and loud noises may actually be painful. Hyperacusis can be caused by medications, head trauma, certain diseases or viruses, and overexposure to loud noises. It is often present with tinnitus, or with auditory processing disorder.

Auditory Processing Disorder: Auditory processing disorder occurs when a child's brain has difficulty appropriately processing incoming sounds, especially language. Children with auditory processing disorder may have perfectly good hearing, but they may transpose words in sentences, or not hear parts of words. They often have trouble sorting out conversation meant for them from background noises. This disorder can be accompanied by other issues, such as autism, dyslexia, and ADHD, but it can also be present on its own.

Selective Hearing: Selective hearing, of course, is not a true hearing disorder, but it can be hard to differentiate selective hearing from true hearing loss. Students with selective hearing do hear and understand you, but are choosing to ignore you.

Sources:
American Academy of Otolaryngology—Head and Neck Surgery (http://www.entnet.org/index.cfm)

National Institutes of Health: National Institute on Deafness and Other Communication Disorders (http://www.nidcd.nih.gov/)

Palo Alto Medical Foundation: Hearing Loss in Children (http://www.pamf.org/hearinghealth/facts/children.html)

Sign Language Alphabet

Use this page to teach students to sign the alphabet.

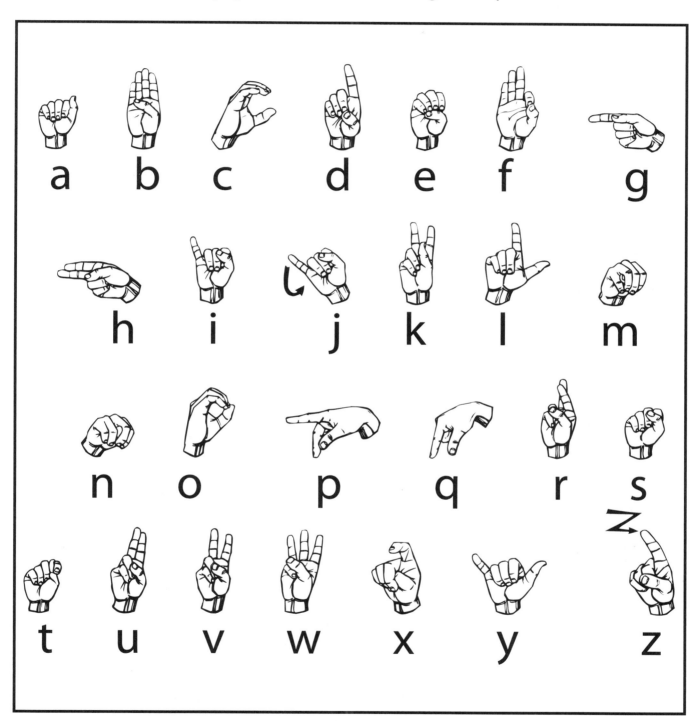

Other Physical Disabilities

Having a classmate with a physical disability can be a great life experience. Rather than modifying student behavior, the goal of this chapter is more about establishing flexible routines and procedures that help the student become a fully participating member of the classroom. This may mean changing what you normally do in order to accommodate that student while still reaching your goals. It also means helping the rest of the class adjust to the new routines and to take part in them.

General Guidelines for Accommodating Students with Physical Disabilities

Physical disabilities (other than hearing or vision loss) come in all shapes and sizes. Some of the ones you are most likely to come across in general classrooms include students with challenges from cerebral palsy, muscular dystrophy, and birth defects like missing or malformed limbs and spina bifida. Also included in this chapter are ideas for students with temporary disabilities from childhood accidents, and students with severe allergies and asthma, since these will definitely affect your classroom routines.

There is a difference between students who are "suddenly" unable to be mobile as the result of an accident, and students who have permanent disabilities. Often, it is more difficult to accommodate a student who has an accident because you do not have time to prepare and change routines accordingly. If there is an accident during the year, try to talk with the parent before the student comes back to school so that you can plan for different ways to get around the school, deal with bathroom issues, and make any other special accommodations to help things continue to run smoothly.

Students who have tested positive for severe allergies or who have asthma are just like all the other students in your classroom—until they come into contact with an allergen and have trouble breathing or break out in severe hives. This can be a life-and-death situation, scary for the student, and for classmates as well. Establishing firm routines is very important, as is preparing for the worst-case scenario.

Tricks and Tips for Dealing with Other Physical Disabilities

Physical Challenges

❖ **If you have a student with a known disability entering your classroom,** interview parents before the school year begins to find out what equipment the student needs, and to gather information about the student's condition and any additional help that is needed. Use the Tell Us about Your Child form (page 34) to find out more about the student's capabilities and needs.

❖ **Students with physical disabilities may feel like objects of curiosity.** The more you, as the teacher, take the disability in stride, the less that student will feel singled out. Give them the extra help they need, but do not show extraordinary favoritism or disfavor. The student does not have to be the line leader every time, nor must he always be the caboose. Make an effort, in other words, to treat that student just like everyone else, and trust that classmates will follow your lead. And remember that the more you expect of the student with a disability, they more they will be able to do.

❖ **Include pictures of students and people with disabilities in your classroom**.

❖ **As much as possible, allow the student to begin transitions earlier** than the rest of the class so that he does not feel rushed. Simple routines like toileting, going outside, putting on coats and jackets, and even visiting the lunchroom or specials rooms can take a lot of time.

❖ **If the student needs a helper, make it a privilege** by turning it into a classroom job. Students love being classroom helpers, and they will look forward to helping the student as much as they will look forward to being the line leader or door holder. Jobs for the student helper can include holding doors, taking notes, writing, cutting, or walking at the pace of the student if he has to move more slowly than others.

- ❖ **If a student cannot write down notes, provide a tape recorder** so that a scribe (either parents or a paraprofessional) can write the notes later. Or, make copies of peer notes for that student to use.

- ❖ **Have the student complete simple writing assignments orally.** For example, if a student must circle the arctic animals on a worksheet, have her point to them instead.

- ❖ **There will probably be times when a student cannot participate in an activity,** and she will be sad about it. For example, you do not want to send a student with a broken leg into a bounce house at the School Carnival. In those situations, give the student a different fun thing to do, such as be the doorkeeper for the bounce house, or get extra computer time later, to make up for the missed activity.

Allergies/Asthma

- ❖ **Use the Tell Us about Your Child form** (page 34) to keep a written record of allergies and asthma triggers in students.

- ❖ **Follow your school's food policy** and make sure that all parents are aware of it. Many students now have severe nut allergies, that many schools have strict policies governing the presence of nuts and peanut butter.

- ❖ **Ask that parents stand firm with their children from the beginning in not allowing allergy foods** (if that is your school's policy) to take the focus off of the classmate with allergies.

- ❖ **If you teach younger students, invite the student's parent to come in and explain** to classmates what the allergy is and what it means. This eliminates the need for young students to explain why they cannot have a cupcake or trade food at lunch.

- ❖ **Ask parents of students with food allergies to send in a goodie box** so that the student can enjoy treats when classmates do.

- ❖ **If you ask parents to send in party treats, send home a list of safe foods.** You may also request small toys instead of foods.

- ❖ **Have the student with allergies use the same place mat and sit in the same chair every day,** labeled with the student's name. Designate these as an "allergen-free" zone.

- ❖ **For even more safety, have the student sit at an allergen-free table.** Tell students that if they want to sit there, they cannot bring allergy foods for lunch. With luck, students will consider it a treat to sit at that table.

- ❖ **Set up strict rules about students keeping hands to themselves.** Do not allow any students to trade food.

- ❖ **EpiPens and nebulizers or inhalers** (sometimes with spacers) are an important part of allergy treatment. It is one thing to read the directions for using these devices, and quite another to stick a child with the pen or help him use the inhaler in an emergency. Have an emergency drill with the parent and the student and pretend to use the pen or the inhaler. Show other teachers how to do this in case you are absent during an emergency. Post the EpiPen/Inhaler Instructions (page 35) in your classroom. (Have a parent show you how to use a nebulizer. It must be battery operated or plugged in and it takes a while to administer medicine this way.)

- ❖ **Regularly check that EpiPens asthma medicines have not expired.**

- ❖ **Monitor students with asthma on the playground and during gym.** Colds, cold weather, stress, crying, and exercise can all bring on an asthma attack.

- ❖ **Asthma attacks can come on slowly and be hard to notice in a noisy environment.** If you suspect a student is having a hard time breathing, listen for coughing first. (It can be the only indicator of asthma.) Then, take the student to a quiet room and listen for wheezing, especially when the student exhales.

- ❖ **Students who are on an antihistamine or other allergy medicine may seem "dopey" or sleepy.** Discuss the student's dosage times with parents so that you can identify times when the student is more likely to be sleepy. If your school permits a rest period, schedule it then. Otherwise, schedule a quiet activity like self-selected reading when you know the student will need some down time, then transition to an active period to help the student wake up a little.

Physical Disabilities Worksheet #1: **Tell Us about Your Child**

Please fill out this sheet for us to keep on file. It will help us give your child the best experience possible by giving us insight about special help your child might need while in school.

Child's Name: _____

Address: _____

City, State, Zip: _____ Phone: _____

Mother's Name: _____ Home Phone (If Different from Above): _____

Work Phone: _____ Cell Phone: _____

Father's Name: _____ Home Phone (If Different from Above): _____

Work Phone: _____ Cell Phone: _____

Emergency Contact: _____ Relationship to Child: _____

Contact's Phone Numbers: _____

Please describe any special help your child needs while at school: _____

_____

_____

- -

Physical Disabilities Worksheet #2: **Tell Us about Your Child**

Please fill out this sheet for us to keep on file. It will help us give your child the best experience possible by giving us insight about special help your child might need while in school.

Child's Name: _____

Address: _____

City, State, Zip: _____ Phone: _____

Mother's Name: _____ Home Phone (If Different from Above): _____

Work Phone: _____ Cell Phone: _____

Father's Name: _____ Home Phone (If Different from Above): _____

Work Phone: _____ Cell Phone: _____

Emergency Contact: _____ Relationship to Child: _____

Contact's Phone Numbers: _____

List of Known Allergens: _____

Typical Reactions: _____

Please describe any special help your child needs while at school: _____

_____

_____

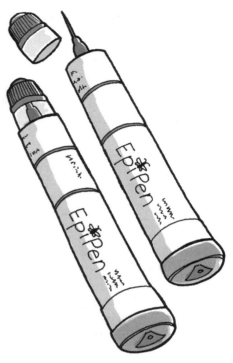

Follow these directions to administer an EpiPen shot.

1. Have someone call 911 immediately.
2. Make a fist around the EpiPen® with one hand.
3. Pull off the GRAY Safety Cap with the other hand. (Do not cover the black tip with part of your hand. If you accidentally inject yourself, go immediately to the emergency room.)
4. Hold the black tip near the student's outer thigh. (It should be against bare skin, but can be injected through clothing if necessary.) The tip should be perpendicular to the student's leg.
5. Have someone hold the student firmly so his leg is still.
6. Jab the black tip firmly into the student's thigh. You should hear a click.
7. Hold the EpiPen firmly in place for 10 seconds, and then remove it from the thigh.
8. Check the black tip. If you see an exposed needle, the injection was successful. If the tip is not exposed, repeat steps 4–7.
9. Gently massage the injection area for several seconds. (It is normal for the student to feel his heart pounding at this time.)
10. Dispose of the EpiPen in a "sharps" container or give the expended EpiPen to paramedics.

Asthma Inhaler with Spacer Instructions

Follow these directions to administer asthma medicine.

A young student will have a spacer that fits over her mouth and nose. An older student may have a mouthpiece on the end of his spacer, or may not need a spacer.

For a mouth-and-nose spacer:

1. Fit the asthma mouthpiece into the hole in the rounded end of the spacer.
2. Gently but firmly hold the mask over the student's mouth and nose.
3. Push down on the top of the inhaler. Instruct the student to breath normally for about six breaths.
4. Repeat if the student's doctor has prescribed a second puff of medicine.

For a mouth-only spacer:

1. Fit the asthma mouthpiece into the hole in the rounded end of the spacer.
2. Help the student put the spacer mouthpiece into his mouth, exhale completely, and close his lips to form a seal.
3. Push down on the top of the inhaler. Instruct the student to breath in through his mouth as deeply as possible.
4. The student should then hold his breath for at least 10 seconds in order to absorb the medicine.
5. Repeat if the student's doctor has prescribed a second puff of medicine.

For an inhaler without a spacer:

1. Help the student put the inhaler mouthpiece into his mouth and close his lips to form a seal.
2. Push down on the top of the inhaler. Instruct the student to take a simultaneous, deep breath through his mouth, and hold his breath as long as possible, for at least 10 seconds.
3. Repeat if the student's doctor has prescribed a second puff of medicine.

Chapter 3
Language and Literacy Development

❖ **limited speech (clarity)** ❖

❖ **limited speech (language acquisition)** ❖

❖ **letter recognition and reading difficulties** ❖

Language and literacy development are two of the most important skills young students acquire. Preschoolers learn to use their words to ask for what they need, and elementary school students learn to read—a must for succeeding in school.

Although preschoolers achieve much of their language acquisition outside of the classroom, preschool is very important to the process of language and literacy development. Long before students actually read their first words, language and literacy are already developing through storytelling, talking with friends, negotiating play, and understanding that those little black marks on a page are letters and words that tell a story. The activities and themes selected by preschool teachers give plenty of opportunity for vocabulary expansion, and story time provides examples of fluency. Of course, elementary teachers will have a smoother road in teaching vocabulary, phonics, phonemic awareness, comprehension, and fluency if students already have a solid language and literacy background in preschool. These teachers will continue to build good language and literacy experiences.

This chapter addresses barriers to language and literacy development. One such barrier is speech clarity. Students who cannot speak clearly will struggle to communicate with their peers and teachers, which can cause great frustration. Another barrier to language development is poor vocabulary. Students must learn enough vocabulary to be able talk about common topics. For example, if you are talking about birds in class, you will have to teach vocabulary like *feathers*, *owl*, and *birdseed* so that students understand what these things are. If you have an ESL student in your classroom who is being bitten by a classmate, you need to make sure the ESL student can say, "Stop biting me!" clearly in English, so he can use his words as a first intervention.

As students progress from speaking and gaining new vocabulary to letter recognition, and then to interest in reading, then to writing letters, reading and writing difficulties may come to light. Using some of the ideas in this book will help start even reluctant students on a developmentally appropriate path to learning these crucial skills.

Limited Speech (Clarity)

It is normal for students to have unclear speech as they learn to talk. Students may also make up their own words for things, which can sounds like clarity of speech issues. There are also certain sounds that naturally develop later than others. (See the Speech Clarity Chart on page 39 for a guide to when sounds develop for most students.) Overall, though, by age four, students should be understandable most of the time. If you cannot understand what a student is saying because his words are not clear, or if classmates play "through" the student's speech rather than engaging with him, you probably need to help him work on his speech.

Indicators of Clarity Problems with Speech

❖ **Talks too fast and slurs words when speaking or reading.** (A student who is reading may slur or gloss over words she cannot yet read or sound out, indicating a developing vocabulary rather than poor speech clarity. Also, good readers may slur words as they transition from reading aloud to silent reading.)

❖ **Mumbles or speaks too quietly to be heard, or fails to make eye contact so that you cannot see their lips forming words.** (This can be a reaction to frustration with classmates and teachers saying, "What?"

❖ **Talks with stiff lips or talks out of the side of the mouths. May also talk with teeth clenched** ("Ventriloquist speaking").

❖ **Stutters when speaking.** (This is different from repeating the beginning of a sentence several times because they are in a hurry or too excited. Students around the age of three and four may make several "false starts" because their mouths are catching up with the explosion of language development that is happening in their brains.)

❖ **Has phonetic issues, like difficulty saying /p/, /f/, /th/.** (This is often associated with hearing loss.)

❖ **Has a pronounced accent due to cultural, regional, or first language influences, that impedes understanding.** (For example, a teacher from the Northeast may have a difficult time understanding a student from the South, and an American teacher may not understand a student with a strong accent influenced by a first language.)

Tricks and Tips for Dealing with Clarity Problems with Speech

❖ **An undiagnosed hearing loss can easily manifest itself in speech clarity issues.** If you notice a student's speech is unclear, try some of the tricks in the poor hearing section (pages 28–31).

❖ **At the beginning of the year, ask parents of very young students if they have noticed a systematic issue with clarity.** For example, if parents tell you that their two-year-old daughter always replaces /th/ with /f/ or /l/ with /w/, you will learn to listen for that replacement and have an easier time understanding it, and you can also devise specific help for learning those letter sounds. (Of course, parents may not hear their children's speech issues, since they live with them and hear them all of the time.)

❖ **Enlist parental help when specific words are problematic.** For example, if a student says a friend's name wrong, ask the parent to gently reinforce the correct pronunciation at home.

❖ **It can be easy to adapt to a student with a pronounced speech difficulty,** meaning that you may eventually begin to understand what the student is saying despite clarity problems. That is necessary for communication in the classroom, but do not gloss over improving his speech. Occasionally ask a fellow teacher to talk to the student to get feedback on how well she understands him, so that you have an objective opinion about whether the student's speech is more clear, or whether you just "know how" to listen to him.

- ❖ **Ask students to repeat what they say, but not more than twice.** Then, ask them to explain or describe what they are saying so that they use different words and you have a better chance of "getting it."

- ❖ **To keep a student from getting frustrated when you do not understand her, make it "your fault."** Ask her to tell you more so that you can understand. Then, she is helping you out instead of doing something wrong.

- ❖ **Repeat the student's words back to him.** If you get it "right," he will be happy that you understand him. If you get it "wrong," he will repeat himself.

- ❖ **Not being understood triggers anger and tears in many students.** They are trying so hard to communicate and it can take all their self-control just to get the words out. Be extra patient with these students when they get frustrated and act out.

- ❖ **Share plenty of books with tongue twisters, rhymes, and alliteration.** Getting students to play with language can be the first key to getting them to talk more often, and then more easily.

- ❖ **Encourage students to record their voices so they can hear themselves talk.** They will be fascinated by the fact that they sound different on tape, and will talk more just to hear themselves.

- ❖ **If you suspect a student is stuttering,** be patient and act as if what she is saying is very important. This is hard to do in a busy classroom, but having a captive audience will give her courage and patience to work through her words.

- ❖ **If a student has trouble getting the words out,** ask him to stop and gather his thoughts before he speaks. Having the words in his head first may help him say them more easily.

- ❖ **Sing with students as often as possible.** Many people who stutter have a much easier time if they sing words.

- ❖ **If a student has a true speech issue, early intervention can be very helpful.** For example, if a student is difficult to understand by about the middle of his fourth year, a referral many be needed. Many public school systems offer speech therapy to preschoolers, and of course there are many private resources, as well. Finally, most students do get some kind of speech screening during their kindergarten evaluations.

- ❖ **Buy a cheap, plastic microphone from a discount store.** Let students take turns performing—they will talk in silly voices and use funny words, and more talking is good in this instance. (See illustration.)

Speech Clarity Chart

Below is a list of speech sounds and the typical ages by which students should master them. No two students will develop at exactly the same time, but if you notice a significant lag in pronouncing some of these sounds, consider having a colleague or a speech language pathologist casually observe your classroom and talk with the student in order to get a second opinion.

Age 3: vowel sounds, b, h, m, n, p, w

Age 4: d, f, g, k, y

Age 5: t, ng

Age 6: ch, j, l, sh

Age 7: r, s, z

Age 8: th, v, zh

Tongue Twisters

Share these tongue-tying tidbits with students.

Shannon shovels snow, sleet, and snails.

Thick socks stick to thin shoes.

Peanut butter brittle's better on a paddle.

Ralphie ran over and Ronnie ran around.

Whales ride waves and wash in the rain.

Lucy loves Lola's little llama, Laura.

Brad banged and broke big brother's bottles.

Limited Speech (Language Acquisition)

Students can have limited vocabularies for a variety of reasons. A second-language speaker is learning to translate as well as talk. A different student may be from another part of the country and use colloquial words or a different syntax or accent. Students with hearing issues, stuttering issues, or auditory processing disorders may have trouble with acquiring vocabulary. If they simply cannot hear new words, or cannot process them, then it is hard for them to turn around and use them in speech. Finally, a student can have a limited vocabulary due to lack of experiences. If student's family members do not spend much time engaging him in meaningful conversations, or are unable to provide a variety of experiences for him that broaden his vocabulary, he does not have opportunities to learn and use new words. In some large families, the student may not be able to get a word in edgewise. It is hard to learn to use new words when you rarely get to talk. (Never getting a chance to talk at home can also cause students to talk constantly at school!)

There are many ways to expand students' vocabularies. Just the experience of school will make this happen, but by structuring lessons and planning conversations, you will be able to introduce students to many new words and give them plenty of chances to practice.

Indicators of Limited Language Acquisition
- ❖ Rarely initiates conversations.
- ❖ Gives one-word answers for most things, with little explanation.
- ❖ Does not raise hand during circle time.
- ❖ Does not like to bring show-and-tell or gets flustered when talking about it.
- ❖ Has trouble describing artwork or telling stories.
- ❖ Uses "tired" words for everything. For example, says she likes all of her friends because they are "nice," but does not volunteer any more information or describe how/why they are nice.
- ❖ Has difficulty writing stories (older students).
- ❖ Has trouble retelling stories. This is a tough skill for younger students in general, but if students do not understand most of the vocabulary, they cannot tell you what happened.

Tricks and Tips for Dealing with Limited Language Acquisition

- ❖ **Again, if a student's language acquisition is behind, recommend a hearing check.**

- ❖ **Reading and retelling stories increase vocabulary.** To teach retelling, stop as you are reading to ask questions about what is happening, what students think will happen next, what they will see in the pictures, and so on.

- ❖ **Ask parents to increase their reading time with students.** Send home the Retelling Worksheet (page 42) for parents to use with their students when reading at home. Ask the parent and student to fill in the sheet together and return it. If you think the work may be challenging for a student, simplify it; cover some of the questions before you make the copy to send home.

- ❖ **Encourage parents to spend mealtime and drive time chatting with their kids,** thus offering chances to expand vocabulary. Even parents who do not speak English are encouraging fluency in general when talking with children.

- ❖ **If students get talked over at home, recommend that family members use the talking stick.** Decorate a stick with paint or streamers. When a student is holding the stick, it is his time to talk.

- ❖ **Have students rehearse show-and-tell before the big day.** Send home the Show-and-Tell Practice Page (page 43) with each student. It reminds parents of show-and-tell day, and also gives them tips for helping a student choose facts to share about his show-and-tell.

- ❖ **Watch out for colloquial language, which can be tricky to spot, but can impede understanding.** For example, if you tell a student to "push" a toy car along the floor and she does not understand what to do, she may need to hear "roll" or "drive" it along the floor.

❖ **Teaching with themes can help support vocabulary acquisition** by exposing students to many related words. As they study the theme, they build a scaffold for even more new words.

❖ **Play the descriptive word game.** When a student uses a common word like *nice* or *pretty*, have students list synonyms for that common word. Words like *kind, friendly,* or *polite* can replace *nice,* while *beautiful, lovely,* or *gorgeous* can replace *pretty*. Let young students tell the words, but write them down for older students.

❖ **Colors can inspire great descriptive vocabulary.** Provide a box of 64 crayons. Let students choose one color group, such as greens. Pull out all of the green crayons. Color a swatch of each green crayon on a piece of chart paper, and write the name next to it: sea foam, chartreuse, mint, etc. Talk about how each color looks like its name. On subsequent days, make charts for the other color groups.

❖ **Travel really broadens students' vocabularies.** If field trips are difficult or too expensive, plan field trips to different parts of your school. Visit the kitchen, a natural area, the worship area (if there is one), staff room, gym, or playground. Make an oral or written list of all of the objects in that area. Talk about the new words with students, and let each student draw a picture of one of the new objects, then tell about his picture.

❖ **Use the Internet or educational videos to take field trips.** Web sites like National Geographic®, historical sites, and sometimes even local Chambers of Commerce may have guided virtual tours of many different places. Treat the videos like books by pausing them to review different words and objects. Keep a list of new words so you can use them in conversations with students.

❖ **As part of the screening process, some kindergartens have incoming students tell as many names of animals as possible in a specific amount of time.** Let students do this with different categories, like vegetables, fruits, favorite cartoon characters, colors, baseball teams, etc. Or, during one-on-one time with a student, show her an object. Let the student spend a couple of minutes describing it using as many adjectives as possible.

Encourage her to use her senses by smelling the object, tasting it (if it is food), touching it, looking at it, and shaking it to see whether it makes a noise. Start with a small amount of time, like three minutes, then add more time.

❖ **Play a movement game.** Tell students to, "Walk quickly!" "Crawl slowly!" Combine different verbs and adverbs as students move across an open space. Students who do not know what some of the words mean will copy those who do. Be sure to repeat the words and let students tell what they mean.

❖ **Place something large in a silly place.** For example, draw a scary face on a balloon and hang it from the ceiling. When students point it out, act as if you have no idea what they mean. Have students give you directional words to find the object. Require older students to use complete sentences to direct you.

❖ **Students recall lyrics easily when singing,** so introduce new songs, rhymes, and chants.

❖ **Do not be afraid to use big words,** like calling spiders *arachnids*, or teaching students about the *Iditarod*. Students love the challenge of big words and will often work extra hard to learn and use them.

I spy an arachnid!

This is a picture of the Iditarod!

Retelling Worksheet

Student's Name: _____   **Date:** _____

Directions: After reading a story with your child, ask her the following questions. Fill in the written answers, and let her draw the pictures. If she is already writing, let her write the answers herself.

What is the title of the book? _____

Who is the author? _____

What are the names of the main characters?	**What happened at the beginning?**
How did the book end?	**What happened in the middle?**
Did you like this book? Why or why not?	**What was your favorite part?**

Show-and-Tell Practice Page

Student's Name: _____ **Show-and-Tell Date:** _____

Directions: Answer these questions about your show and tell item.

1. Tell the name of the item you brought for show-and-tell. _____

    _____

2. Talk about what size it is. _____

    _____

    _____

3. What color is it? Name something else that is the same color. _____

    _____

4. Why did you bring it in? _____

    _____

    _____

    _____

5. Does it have moving parts? Please show us how it works. _____

    _____

    _____

Letter Recognition and Reading Difficulties

Kindergarten expectations can seem like a far leap from preschool expectations. In many elementary schools, students are now expected to read before the end of kindergarten. Obviously, not every child will end her preschool career ready to read and write. This is one reason for the trend of holding children out of kindergarten until they are six, having them attend readiness, or having them repeat kindergarten.

Most students can start recognizing letters around age four. By ages four and five, students should be ready to learn letters. Some students are ready to learn letter sounds, and many students are ready to read by age five. But, capability does not always equal interest. When students start showing interest in letters, they will willingly engage in literacy activities. Learning to read is a very individual process; a child who is not interested in reading may simply enjoy other things or have other strengths. Because reading is the foundation for all academic learning, any ground students gain in literacy before kindergarten will give them a boost when the hard work begins.

Indicators and Signs of Letter Recognition and Reading Difficulties

❖ **Struggles with "handedness" past age four or so.** Not having chosen a "hand" yet can keep students from learning left-to-right progression, and from training hand muscles to write.

❖ **Has difficulty crossing the midline.** May start writing from right to left. May write or read backwards. (In older students, this can indicate dyslexia or eye issues, as well.)

❖ Cannot recognize that certain marks and scribbles are letters or numbers.

❖ **Regularly transposes letters.** For example, if you teach the number 45, a student may call it 54, or turn the number upside down.

❖ **May have speech issues.** (Students who cannot master phonics can also have a hard time speaking or reading aloud.)

❖ **Does not seek out the class book center or enjoy the media center.** May flip through several books in quick succession, or disrupt classmates who are engaged.

❖ **Uses evasive tactics to hide poor reading skills.** Asks to go to the restroom, complains of stomachache or headache, acts out during reading time, never raises hand, forgets homework, repeats others' answers.

❖ Shows signs of stress when asked to read.

Tricks and Tips for Dealing with Letter Recognition and Reading Difficulties

❖ **Let students "air write:"** write with a finger in the air.

❖ **Make textured letters.** Cut them from sandpaper or fabric, or have students write in sand, mud, pudding, or shaving cream.

❖ **Purchase pencil grips** or fat pencils to train little hands to grip pencils correctly.

❖ **Provide plenty of alphabet books,** as well as books of tongue twisters that celebrate alliteration.

❖ **Designate a different letter of the day or week,** and celebrate it. For example, if the letter of the week is A, let Adam and Ashanti be class helpers.

Ask students to bring in show-and-tell items that start with A. Have a letter A snack, such as applesauce.

❖ **Let students help you cut out bulletin board letters.**

❖ **Go on a letter scavenger hunt.** Give each student an uppercase or lowercase letter cutout. Take students on a trip around the school until every student finds a matching letter or object that begins with that letter.

❖ **Post bulletin board paper around the room.** Let students paint letters with big brushes.

- ❖ **Provide outlines of letters on heavy paper.** Have each student cut out a letter and then cut out three magazine pictures that match that letter. Have the student glue the letter and pictures on paper to make a collage.

- ❖ **Remind students that they are working hard,** especially as they learn letters like *g* and *c*, which have more than one primary sound.

- ❖ **Give each student a letter cutout of the first letter in his first name.** Have students use the letters to line up in alphabetial order.

- ❖ **Tracing is a good exercise for all ages,** since it teaches letters and also help students practice their handwriting and tone their hand muscles. Have young students trace the letters on the Letter Tracing page (page 46).

- ❖ **Let students choose the letters they want to learn.** Ask a student to name his favorite place or toy, then make that letter the letter of the week. For example, if a student says his favorite toy is his pirate ship, make *p* the letter of the week, and play pirates in class. Each week, let students make letter books using the Letter Book reproducible (page 47). Students should draw the letter of the week on the front and then follow the directions to complete the book.

- ❖ **As students start reading, fall back on the Reading Recovery strategy.** Let students read through books without worrying about getting all of the words right. This helps them build confidence, since they do not constantly worry about getting it wrong.

- ❖ **Play "reading time" like you would play school.** Let a student be in charge of selecting a book for the group, talking about it, and helping read it to the class.

- ❖ **If you have video-hungry students, read a book and then watch the video,** then compare the two. Make a list of ways the book and video are alike and different.

- ❖ **Share a favorite book several times.** This gives students a chance to memorize it and then "read" it.

- ❖ **Invite guest readers** in to heighten interest during story time.

- ❖ **Tell a story with pictures.** If a student has a hard time with reading, ask her parents to let her tell the story using the pictures instead of reading the words. Tell parents not to insist on getting the story "right." Creative license is fine!

- ❖ **Do not confine reading to books;** use other print material. For example, show a student a word on a grocery list and let him look for it in the housekeeping area. Or, let students read signs around the school.

- ❖ **Take advantage of environmental print** with the usual things (signs, grocery items) but also focus on things that students are interested in: video game names, character names, their family members' names, etc.

- ❖ **Teach them how to spell the number words** and match them to numerals.

- ❖ **Make a letter-accomplished wall.** As students master different letters, post them on the wall or a bulletin board. Celebrate every new letter the students learn.

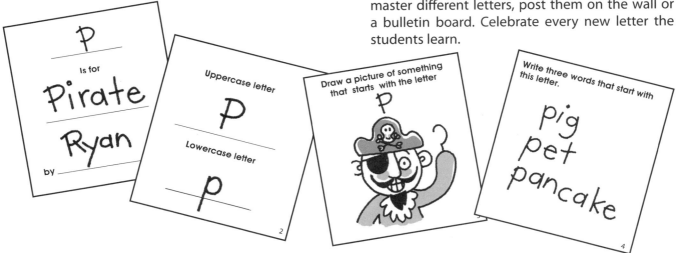

Letter Tracing

Student's Name: _____ **Date:** _____

Directions: Follow the dots to trace the letters.

A B C D E F
G H I J K L
M N O P Q R S
T U V W X Y Z

a b c d e f
g h i j k l
m n o p q r s
t u v w x y z

Letter Book

Directions: Follow the directions to make a letter book. When you finish, cut out the pages and staple them together.

    Page 1. Write the letter and a word that begins with that letter.

    Page 2. Write the uppercase and lowercase letter.

    Page 3. Draw a picture of something that starts with that letter.

    Page 4. Write three words that start with that letter.

_____

Is for

_____

by _____

Uppercase letter

_____

Lowercase letter

_____

2

Draw a picture of something that starts with the letter

_____.

3

Write three words that start with this letter.

4

Chapter 4
Attention Span

❖ inability to sit still (circle time or morning meeting) ❖
❖ inability to play at something for a length of time (center time) ❖
❖ inability to stay on task (table or seatwork) ❖

Teachers and parents alike hear the phrase "ready to learn" a lot. Teachers use it as a command to get their students to settle down, pay attention, and get ready to work. The phrase is also used to describe a student who has certain skills that will enable her to absorb information. That's why the "bridge class" between preschool and kindergarten is called "readiness."

However, many things can work against young students being ready to learn in kindergarten and then elementary school. For one thing, kindergarten students spend much more time sitting still and working at a table, as every teacher knows and every parent finds out when worksheets start coming home and their children share that they spent almost no time playing in housekeeping and with blocks. Also, because of increasingly busy work and activity schedules, families may spend far less time sitting down for dinner and conversation, playing games, or reading together. Add the pull of video games and television, and you have children who do not concentrate on tasks for any great length of time, and therefore have not yet learned to sit still and do work.

As you teach students who have trouble paying attention, remember that these students need plenty of kindness, patience, and compassion; often, they need even more than their quieter peers. Some are trying hard to get attention they need, some may have ADHD and will require more extensive help, and some students truly just do not understand typical school behavior expectations. These students will respond to your patience, kindness, consistency, and firmness.

Inability to Sit Still
(Circle Time or Morning Meeting)

Circle time, or morning meeting, is an important part of preschool and early elementary school. It is the time when teachers teach calendar skills, acknowledge birthdays and holidays, discuss weather, read stories, and give announcements. Think if it as the precursor to sitting in a departmental meeting. It is when students learn to take turns speaking, respect others who are talking, and learn self-control. Most teachers have at least one student who interrupts the morning meeting every day. Because seating arrangements during this time are often unstructured, it can be very difficult for some students to resist touching and bothering classmates, and to keep their hands and bodies under control. Remember that for young students, and especially for students with certain disabilities, sitting still and paying attention during group activities is truly difficult. Starting in kindergarten, students are expected to sit still for long periods of time, so exercise patience and kindness as you help students learn a measure of self-control.

Indicators of Inability to Sit Still During Circle Time or Morning Meeting
- ❖ Rolls around on floor or rocks back and forth.
- ❖ Is unable to sit crisscross applesauce.
- ❖ Constantly moves hands and feet.
- ❖ Disturbs neighbors by crowding or touching them.
- ❖ Talks to self and others.
- ❖ Sighs a lot, rolls eyes, makes faces, or otherwise indicates that sitting still is not fun.
- ❖ Picks at clothes, scabs, hair, underwear, or carpet.
- ❖ Touches nearby toys.

Tips and Tricks to Helps Students Sit Still During Circle Time or Morning Meeting

- ❖ **Plan your circle time or morning meeting area away from obvious distractions** like toys and bookshelves. If you cannot move the meeting area, hang a curtain that you can pull over distractions.

- ❖ **Use carpet squares or tape to designate spaces for students to sit on.** If you need to mark boundaries, use hoops on the floor.

- ❖ **Address the problem before it starts.** Make a chart with your rules for sitting in morning meeting. Read the rules each morning until students can recite them from memory.

- ❖ **Experts recommend enforcing one minute of time-out for each year of age.** Modify that graduated system for morning meetings. Do not expect three-year-olds to sit more than ten minutes, and add five minutes per year of age. This does not mean that they cannot sit longer than that, but giving them frequent breaks will yield much better results.

- ❖ **Students have a much easier time paying attention in the morning** than they do in the afternoon, when they are getting tired. Schedule your circle time in the morning. (You may also have another circle time later in the day for reading.)

- ❖ **Clearly define transitions.** Young students often struggle with transitions, maybe because they do not want to end a fun activity, or because the uncertainty between activities is frustrating. Elementary students need to adjust to frequent stops and starts; math does not blend into reading, and lunch does not blend in with art. Reinforce this by having clear transition times between activities. You can play music during transition times so that students have a clear stop and start time while they clean up, put away, and come to sit quietly with their classmates.

- ❖ **Act the part.** Have your assistant sit with students and bother them in any of the various ways mentioned above. Let students tell you what the assistant is doing to disrupt circle time.

- ❖ **Do not wait until the wiggles start to get rid of them.** Turn on some music and let students dance and wiggle for a couple of minutes before sitting down for a meeting or work period.

- ❖ **Teach students to sit on the floor crisscross applesauce.** Sitting this way gives students a firm base that makes it harder to rock or move. If you need to, correctly position students until they can do it on their own.

- ❖ **If students prefer to sit up on their knees,** allow that position as well, since crisscross applesauce can be uncomfortable for some students, while others are short and may do this in order to see over classmates. (Students who sit on their knees should sit in the back of the group, and smaller students should sit in front.)

- ❖ **For a student who really cannot control himself, provide a chair in the back of the circle or meeting area.** Let that student sit in the chair; it will act as a natural boundary as long as he is able to stay in it. Be matter-of-fact when other students ask questions: "The chair helps Nathan sit still while we have our meeting."

- ❖ **Use a rocking chair** for an older student who cannot sit still and may find the movement of the rocking chair soothing.

- ❖ **If adding a chair does not work, let that student move from the meeting to do something else** that is productive, but separate. Do not let the student disrupt the meeting, but be flexible.

- ❖ **Certain disabilities truly prevent students from being still and focused for very long.** The student will become frustrated and his classmates will begin to single him out if you are too insistent, but you can have some reasonable expectations. For example, if you expect classmates to sit still for 15 minutes, excuse that student after 10 minutes until he is able to remain for the rest of the meeting.

- ❖ **Introduce movement and interaction into circle time.** Have students react physically to a story, or read along with repeating story elements. If the story is about music, pause to let them play instruments or pretend to drum on their knees. Have volunteers change calendar dates or move weather symbols.

- ❖ **Also use interaction to call back students who are sighing and daydreaming.** Letting them participate gives students more incentive to focus, since it might be their turn next.

- ❖ **Sometimes, a student is fine at meeting time unless she sits with a certain buddy.** Draw their attention to the fact that they can usually sit still unless they are sitting together. Then, ask what choice they should make when deciding where to sit in morning meeting. Let students have the opportunity to police themselves and sit apart during this time. Assigned seats will also take care of the issue, but especially for older students, it is important to give them a chance to be responsible and make the right choice.

- ❖ **You can tell a lot about a student from how long she can sit still,** and what movements she starts to make. Do not forget to make observations during this time, or ask an assistant to help while you lead the group.

- ❖ **Require students to raise their hands** before giving an answer or asking a question. This keeps one student from dominating discussions.

- ❖ **Remember that some kids are just naturally more active and require more social interaction.** Give those kids a "good job" as often as you can when they deserve it. Immediate, positive feedback is important.

- ❖ **Let students teach themselves and you about sitting still.** Let younger students circle students with good behavior on the Who Is Sitting Still worksheet (page 51). Older students can draw good behavior on the When Do You Sit Still? worksheet (page 52).

- ❖ **Use nonverbal signals to calm boisterous students.** Tap your feet on the floor, stop reading until the student is sitting still and paying attention, turn off the lights, clear your throat, raise your eyebrows, shake your head "no," or put a finger to your lips when a student is talking in circle. Hold the position until he is quiet.

- ❖ **If the issue is keeping hands to herself, give the student something soft to hold** that does not encourage her to interact, like a handkerchief, squishy ball, or piece of yarn. Handling the material may give her enough quiet stimulation to sit still for a longer time.

- ❖ **Finally, do not forget that these are children! They need plenty of active time.** It is unrealistic to expect even elementary students to sit still constantly. They need chances to be loud, wiggly, and silly, to make up for the times when they must sit still. They also need lots of time to socialize—an important part of school. If they have plenty of outlets for activity, it is easier for them to quiet down when the time comes.

Who Is Sitting Still?

Student's Name: _____ **Date:** _____

Directions: Circle the students who are sitting quietly.
What are the other students doing?   Tell your teacher about it.

When Do You Sit Still?

Student's Name: _____ **Date:** _____

Directions: When do you sit still at school? Draw four pictures of yourself sitting still at school. You can be in different rooms and different places.

Inability to Play at Something for a Length of Time
(Center Time)

Preschool center time is often very different from kindergarten and elementary school center time. Preschool centers are designed for structured free play inside. Students may choose between centers, but teacher-selected center materials direct the play. Often, the teacher observes, rather than participates. Elementary school centers are more likely to be teacher directed and academically oriented. They may not even be called *centers,* and they may not last beyond kindergarten. There may be specific activities for students to complete. The teacher may stay with the group, and activities may be group-oriented, or students may work independently within them to complete academic tasks.

The importance of preschool center play cannot be overstated. During center time, students build foundations for appropriate social interaction. They role-play what they see adults doing (good or bad!). They also create problems and then negotiate solutions. And, they play with things at school they may not be allowed to play with at home; boys may play with dolls, and all students get to push the buttons on the (toy) microwave or control the (pretend) television remote. Finally, students learn plenty of self-help skills (table setting, buttoning and tying, dressing, washing and even ironing) while in centers.

When students cannot learn to engage themselves in preschool centers, their future learning in elementary centers may also be affected because they do not learn to concentrate for any length of time. If a student flits from one center to another, or if they "dump and depart"—empty buckets of items in a center without playing with them—it can be a sign of immaturity or inability to focus. The inability to play for a while can alert teachers to a need to observe the student more closely. The student who cannot play in a center may also be the student rolling around on the carpet at story time. She may not appear to have any interests that focus her attention, or be unable to play alone without looking to someone to direct the play. A student who cannot direct her own play, or focus as much as other children, needs extra help in order to develop focus and attention.

Indicators of Inability to Play at Something for a Length of Time (Center Time)

❖ **Constantly roams around the room. Does not seem to know what to do with himself.**
❖ **Is not interested in toys long enough to play with them. Gets out a toy, then abandons it.**
❖ **Dumps out bins of objects without using them. (Dumping is normal for young preschoolers, but older students are usually more purposeful in their play.)**
❖ **Agitates friends who are trying to play. (Knocks over their towers, hoards crayons or other materials.)**
❖ **May sit in the center without playing.**
❖ **May only be comfortable in one center; for example, even though you assign a student to the block center, you keep finding her in the reading center.**
❖ **Prefers the computer center, reading center, or listening center—may not like interaction with classmates.**
❖ **Constantly says things like, "Look at this," or "Can you help me?" so that the teacher affirms their activities. Is not confidant and needs to check in.**
❖ **Reluctance to play may sometimes be cultural. Students from different countries may not know how to play with unfamiliar toys and especially games.**
❖ **May not complete center activities, such as worksheets, coloring assignments, or other tasks.**

Tricks and Tips for Dealing with Inability to Play at Something for a Length of Time (Center Time)

❖ **Set consistent expectations for how long to be in a center.** Insist that students remain in a center until a timer goes off.

❖ **Create a system for how students know to move from one center to another.** This keeps center play fresh and makes sure students encounter a variety of play experiences.

- **Demonstrate imaginative play.** For example, make a pot into a hat or a blanket into a cape. If a student plays with something in a way that it is not usually meant to be played with, let them, unless it is dangerous or inappropriate. Finding new uses for things is the height of creativity, and if you frequently criticize how a student does something in a center, she will start to feel as if she cannot do anything right.

- **When a teacher plays with something in a center,** that toy is "blessed" and every student will want to play with it. Entice a student who has trouble with focusing into the center by offering him that toy.

- **Choose a center to showcase,** and bring out materials from that center for students to play with at tables or in different areas. Once a student experiences and enjoys a new object, he will seek it out when it is back in the center.

- **You can also "bless" an elementary-level center by spending time in it with a few students.** Station yourself or a volunteer or assistant at a center and work one-on-one with a few students each day. Guided reading, retelling, writing, sorting, and skip counting all make great interactive center activities. Students are much more likely to focus when interacting with an adult.

- **Even though they are for "older" students, elementary centers should be fun and engaging.** Use fun paper and markers for writing. Cover books with colorful fabric covers. Supply centers with age-appropriate, interesting counters like rubber band bracelets, toy cars, or some of the tiny-scale toys that are now popular. Supply a popcorn snack while studying popcorn words. Be creative and students will be more engaged.

- **If you find yourself pressed for time to teach anything but elementary math and reading, bring in science and social studies centers.** Science centers can include bubble solutions to test, magnifying glasses and cool objects, and even star stickers, dark paper, and chalk for making constellations. Stock social studies centers with map puzzles, books about your home state or province, or community helper figures. Match the materials to that week's reading if you want things to be connected.

- **If a student's behavior is too disruptive,** sit near the center to encourage better behavior from the student.

- **Sometimes students seem to "forget themselves" when they misbehave.** Adhere a plastic mirror to the wall at student height in the center. If a student catches a glimpse of his own reflection, it may remind him to behave.

- **It may help to pair a shy or reluctant student with a friendly buddy** to make center time more appealing. The comfort level that comes from spending time with a friend can keep a student's attention during play. (Try not to put two very quiet students together. Put a bossy student with one who likes to follow, or a friendly child with a reserved one, so that each student can play to his strengths.)

- **If a reluctant or unfocused student likes race cars, pirates, elephants, or anything else specific, provide related objects to fit each center.** For example, you can provide race car dishes and driver uniforms in housekeeping, books about race cars in the reading center, and cars and tracks in the block center.

- **If students decide to take one center item in another center, let them.** This is counter to the instructions often given to teachers when setting up centers, but it can help students learn to enjoy and focus in other centers.

- **To attract a student to a center, do something unusual,** like adding a tent to the book center, or a stack of shoeboxes to the block center.

- **If several students avoid a center, the center may need some work.** If a student who is always engaged seems suddenly bored, change the supplies in the center. This rule holds especially true in a Readiness class, where you need to make play time more mature to match the higher expectations for students.

- **Do not plan centers blindly. Get to know your students' preferences with the Play Questionnaire** (page 55), then plan your centers with the Center Planning form (page 56). (You can send the questionnaire home or have older students fill it out in class.) Looking back over questionnaires will tell you where to go next, and reviewing center planning pages will simplify things for the next year.

Play Questionnaire

Student's Name: _____ **Date:** _____

Directions: Answer the questions below. Tell about what you like to play.

1. What is your favorite thing to play with at school? _____

_____

2. What is your favorite special activity or center? Why? _____

_____

_____

3. List your three favorite toys that you play with at home.

_____   _____   _____

4. Write the title of your favorite book to read. _____

_____

5. When you play pretend, what do you pretend about? _____

_____

6. If you could receive any toy or game as a gift, what would it be? _____

_____

7. What do you want to learn about in school? _____

_____

_____

Center Planning Form

Teacher Name: _____ **Date:** _____

Center: _____	Center: _____	Center: _____
Theme: _____	Theme: _____	Theme: _____
New Materials:	New Materials:	New Materials:
Date Added:	Date Added:	Date Added:
Date Removed:	Date Removed:	Date Removed:
Center: _____	Center: _____	Center: _____
Theme: _____	Theme: _____	Theme: _____
New Materials:	New Materials:	New Materials:
Date Added:	Date Added:	Date Added:
Date Removed:	Date Removed:	Date Removed:

Inability to Stay on Task
(Table Work or Seatwork)

Table work or seatwork is the basis for much of the work students will do throughout the rest of their school careers. While table work starts out with two- and three-year-olds exploring play dough and manipulatives, it turns into art, writing, file folder games, board games, and even worksheets by the end of preschool and into kindergarten. By first grade, students are expected to complete plenty of table work, both in small groups and individually, and at actual tables or with desks pushed together. And of course, table work will eventually include testing.

While some students find the clearly defined space of a chair and a table comforting, some active students may feel confined. Focus issues really show up during table work when students are often responsible for completing more involved tasks. To help students conquer any problems that they have during table time, use these tricks to enrich table work experiences even for students who do not have trouble focusing.

Indicators of Inability to Stay on Task During Table or Seatwork
❖ **Leans back in chair or rocks desk.**
❖ **Falls off chair.**
❖ **Drops materials.**
❖ **Cannot keep hands still (pokes friends, taps hands).**
❖ **Disrupts neighbors by talking to them or aggravating them.**
❖ **Has trouble sharing materials. (Students get creative about this, and it is often a power struggle. For example, she may try to control community supplies, like a bucket of crayons, by holding one crayon and not allowing anyone else to use it.)**
❖ **Does exceptionally messy work.**
❖ **Cannot follow directions to complete table work.**
❖ **Copies other students because he is unsure of directions.**
❖ **Cannot complete work in a timely fashion.**

Tricks and Tips for Dealing with Inability to Stay on Task During Table or Seatwork

❖ **Morning is an ideal time for table work that requires a lot of concentration.** Students are alert in the morning, and may be tired and sleepy or rowdy in the afternoon.

❖ **Let students start table work as they come into school.** Table activities are a good transition between arriving at school and starting other work. They can help students settle down.

❖ **Afternoon table work should be busy and active,** and encourage student interaction, in order to keep them awake and engaged.

❖ **Even adults have a hard time paying attention for a long time with no mental breaks.** Make table work sessions relatively short and intersperse them with discussion or bathroom and water breaks.

❖ **Have a teacher or assistant sit near a student who has trouble paying attention** to discourage talking and being silly. Or, seat that student with classmates who work quietly so that he has less encouragement to misbehave.

❖ **Place mats can help define each student's table space** and limit classmates from disturbing each other.

❖ **Make sure you have plenty of supplies for table activities.** Young students will fight over the one yellow crayon, and even older students will become frustrated with waiting too long for the glue stick.

❖ **Table work in preschool helps students transition** from working and playing in a group to completing tasks independently. Make sure your table tasks and the directions that go with them are age-appropriate so that students can accomplish some things on their own and are less likely to become frustrated. Consider giving picture directions, simplifying directions for younger students, and having students repeat directions back to you to check their understanding before they start table work.

❖ **Pair a student who has trouble completing table work with a classmate who is a good listener.** The pair can work on following sets of directions together until the student is confident enough to work independently.

❖ **Assign table work based on the preferences of your students who have trouble completing it.** For example, if a student excels in writing but has a hard time with math, assign journal entries for table work and save math for small groups and the whole class. You can learn more about students' table work preferences using the Table Work Ideas page (page 59).

❖ **Alternately, let students choose their own table work.** One student may choose to work on a math assignment, while another student may choose free reading time, and still another student could draw a picture of her completed science experiment. Self-selecting these activities gives control back to students and will help hold their interest.

❖ **It never hurts to go over the rules.** Read the Table Rules reproducible (page 60) to young students, and let older students read and answer their own copies.

❖ **Even for elementary students, table work can be fun.** Let students work on fun art projects, build cooperatively, work together to count to large numbers, or explore items from nature with magnifying glasses.

Table Work Ideas

Student's Name: _____ **Date:** _____

Directions: Draw a picture of something you would like to do at table time.
Write or tell three reasons why you chose this.

Table Rules

Student's Name: _____ **Date:** _____

Directions: What are some of the rules for working at the tables? Read the rules.
Circle the ones you should follow. Draw an X over the ones you should not follow.

1. You should work quietly.

2. Grab things from your friends.

3. Raise your hand if you have a question.

4. Share supplies with your friends.

5. Wiggle in your seat.

6. Kick your friend's chair.

7. Work neatly.

8. Scribble all over your paper.

9. Do not listen to your teacher.

10. Daydream.

11. Drop things on the floor.

12. Try your best.

Chapter 5

Independence and Personal Responsibility

❖ trouble with following directions ❖
❖ trouble retaining information ❖
❖ disorganization ❖

Preschoolers and even kindergartners often come to school still very dependent on Mommy and Daddy for many things. When parents do things like pick out clothing, tie shoes, clean up messes, and constantly remind their children to do tasks (only to eventually give in and do it for them), their children lack independence, responsibility, and the ability to help themselves. In kindergarten and elementary school, students must assume a considerable amount of responsibility for self-help skills. Students have to be able to open their own lunch containers and keep up with their belongings. And, students quickly become responsible for remembering homework assignments, and keeping up with permission slips, progress reports, and other paperwork as it moves from school to home.

Obviously, students who are already able to independently do these and other important tasks have a huge advantage when they start elementary school. The ideas in this chapter are for preschool teachers who want to give their students these self-help advantages, and for elementary teachers who teach students who are not quite there yet, but should be.

Trouble with Following Directions

In preschool, most directions are given orally. Oral directions with multiple steps can be hard for students to follow. Eventually, directions with pictures (prereading directions) are most common. As students learn to read, written directions are more common, both with and without pictures. Even with written directions in front of them, some students just cannot manage to do what their teachers ask without lots of prompting. Many teachers report that having to repeat directions constantly is one of the most frustrating parts of the job. For students, the feeling of missing a step or forgetting what they are supposed to be doing causes a lot of anxiety.

There are several "kinds" of not following directions. There are students who do not hear you. There are students who hear you but do not understand. There are students who understand you, but cannot make it through the directions without getting distracted. Finally, there are students who hear and understand you, but choose to ignore you. As you find out which categories students fall into, you will know more about how to address the problem.

Finally, remember that the goal of learning to follow directions goes beyond getting students to do what you say. When a student can listen and understand directions and then follow them with minimal help, that student has learned self-sufficiency and responsibility—two things that are crucial for success in school and life.

Indicators of Trouble with Following Directions
- ❖ Is the last person to do what you ask.
- ❖ Stands around looking to see what classmates are doing.
- ❖ Does not look at you when you give directions.
- ❖ Seems fearful or hesitant to complete tasks because he is not sure of what to do.
- ❖ Says, "What?" or "Huh?" or "I forgot," a lot.
- ❖ Asks a lot of questions about simple directions. May seem to be avoiding completing them.
- ❖ Whines or says "I can't do it!" about tasks you know she is perfectly capable of completing.

Tricks and Tips for Trouble with Following Directions

- ❖ **If a student really seems lost, check (again) for vision or hearing problems,** including auditory processing disorder. Either issue can make it difficult for students to do what you ask.

- ❖ **Before you give directions,** make sure you have students' undivided attention and full eye contact.

- ❖ **Ask for more attention in degrees.** When you notice some students not paying attention, say something like, "All of our friends are not listening," to give them a chance to do so before you have to start using names.

- ❖ **Seat the student who has a hard time with directions** near where you usually stand to give directions.

- ❖ **Make directions age-appropriate.** Use short, one-step commands for young students, and break long directions into several steps.

- ❖ **Picture cues can help.** Add pictures to sets of directions for washing hands, going to centers, and for anything else that gives students trouble with following directions.

- ❖ **Turning off the lights, ringing a bell,** or saying, "Time to listen," or "Freeze and look at me," are all good signals to get students' attention.

- ❖ **Hand motions can double as visual cues to emphasize your directions.** For example, you may want students to put papers in their folders, then place folders in the backpacks, then line up backpacks in the hallway. As you give these directions, hold up papers, then a folder, then a student backpack, then point out to the hallway. The motions will reinforce your words.

- ❖ **Have a student repeat each step** in a list of directions back to you. (The student who repeats the directions does not necessarily need to be the student who has trouble following them. Sometimes, simply hearing them again from a classmate is enough.)

❖ **When you have a hunch that a student does not know what to do next,** ask a couple of students who do know to repeat the directions, and only then ask the student who does not know. She will have had two more chances to absorb the information.

❖ **Not knowing what to do causes panic in some students,** and can even get in the way of their listening. If they are afraid to ask questions or make mistakes, they may be too fearful to listen well. Asking students to raise their hands if they do not understand can backfire, since students often do not want to be singled out in this way. Watch for a student who seems hesitant while others are getting busy following directions, then have a quiet conversation with that student, who probably needs additional help.

❖ **If you have a student who is capable but unwilling to do what you ask, having a talk with that student may help.** It can help to differentiate between "can't" and "won't" follow directions. Emphasize that you know she can follow directions, and you want to see her do well. Ask, "What would help you follow directions better?" Use some of her suggestions. Making the student a partner in her own success will give her some control, and may get better results.

❖ **Some students need more time to reflect and act,** so give them a chance to succeed by allowing a little extra time for them to do what you ask.

❖ **Remember that moving from listening to directions to following them is a transition,** and transitions are hard. Treat directions like you would any other transition. Establish a warning period (get ready to listen) a listening period, and an action period. Make these transitions clear so students can complete them successfully.

❖ **Use the Picture Directions worksheet (page 64) to help very young students understand a set of directions** you hand out for table work, and to encourage working independently. Provide all of the supplies (paper, crayons, scissors, clips, and a clothesline for displaying artwork). Students should read each step of the directions, then draw a corresponding picture. Check their work for accuracy.

❖ **Elementary students should be able to complete table directions easily;** it is the careful reading that can trip them up. Give each student a copy of the Silly Directions (page 65). Watch them do all of the silly things on the page, then realize that there is a reason some of their classmates are sitting down. Follow this activity with a lesson on how important it is to know everything you need to know before starting some assignments.

Picture Directions

Read or listen to the directions.   Follow the directions to complete the work.

1. **Get a piece of paper and your crayons.**

2. **Draw and color a picture of yourself on the paper.**

3. **Find a pair of safety scissors.**

4. **Cut out the picture you drew.**

5. **Write your name on the back of the picture.**

6. **Ask your teacher for some clips or clothespins.**

7. **Use the clips to hang your artwork on the display string.**

Silly Directions

Directions: Read ALL of the directions on this page before you do any work.

1. Scratch your head.

2. Tap out a rhythm on your knees.

3. Cover your eyes with your hands and count to three.

4. Cross and uncross your legs a few times.

5. Write your middle name here: _____

6. Stand up and SMILE!

7. Sit in your seat and pretend you are dancing to your favorite music.

8. Wave at your neighbor.

9. Flap your arms like a giant bird.

10. Write the date here: _____

11. Rub your hands together.

12. Write your favorite food here: _____

13. Pretend you are cold and shiver.

14. Now that you have finished reading all of the directions, do not do any of them. Sit still and wait.

Trouble Retaining Information

Here it is, six months into the year, and Reid is still forgetting to put his lunch box in his cubbie. Or, Claire cannot remember that her homework needs to go in her homework folder and not crumpled up in her backpack. Or, you find yourself saying, "Eliza, please wash your hands," as she continues to forget to wash her hands when arriving at school. You tell certain students the same things over and over, but very little seems to "stick."

Failure to retain information is a common problem. Since retaining information becomes extremely important in elementary school (say, in testing situations), students need to learn to pay attention and remember what they are told in order to be successful. Helping them master this skill will go a long way toward helping them be successful in school.

Indicators of Trouble with Retaining Information
- Cannot remember simple routines or put belongings in the correct space, even after multiple reminders.
- Does not seem to "register" when asked to do something.
- May not seem engaged with the environment around them.
- Loses or forgets homework, lunch box, etc.
- Cannot find things in the classroom.
- Has trouble navigating what should be familiar routes. For example, cannot remember how to get to the gym or office long after other students have figured it out.
- Constantly looking for clues from classmates about where to go and what to do.
- For older students, cannot remember sight words, master skip counting, or memorize math facts.

Tricks and Tips for Trouble with Retaining Information

- **At the beginning of the year, make reviewing rules and routines part of your daily schedule.** Use the Routine Teacher (page 68) to help students learn and absorb new routines. Write each step of the new routine in each panel and let students illustrate the panels and refer to them until the routine is automatic.

- **Remind yourself that even though you are completely familiar with your way of doing things, to students, your methods are all new.** Remembering this will help you be much more patient.

- **At the beginning of the year, give students ample time to follow directions,** so that those who operate at a slower pace have a chance to respond before getting in trouble.

- **After you give directions, have a student repeat them back to you.** Choose a different student each time so that all students have to pay attention in case they are called on, and the second reminder will help the student who forgets as well as the speaker.

- **Avoid changing routines, and when you do, give plenty of notice.**

- **If you find a student truly cannot recall routines, examine the routines carefully, and pick your battles.** Is it really necessary to have students use a check-in system each morning instead of calling the class roll? If a student hurries back to the classroom every day and forgets to visit the water fountain, is it too disruptive to allow a quick visit later?

- **When giving information or directions, get to the point quickly** and leave out any extraneous information that might confuse students.

- **Post routine reminders around the classroom.** For example, make a large sign (picture or word) over the place where students store their lunches. Tape up a sign to the doorway that asks, "Do you have your coat?" The routine reminders give students opportunities to remind themselves of tasks they are supposed to do.

- **Ask parents to post routine reminder signs at home, or to adopt some routines similar to yours** (like putting away lunch boxes first thing upon arriving home), to reinforce classroom routines.

- **Ask students specific questions.** Any time you ask students questions about what they just read or learned, what they did over the weekend, what a classmate just shared for show-and-tell, or what they liked about a particular class visitor, they will get needed practice in retaining and recalling information.

- **Adjust things for a student who has real difficulty with recall.** For example, when you give the class ten spelling words, assign only five to that student.

- **A student who frequently does not get enough sleep or who misses breakfast can have a very hard time struggling through the day, much less having the wherewithal to remember a classroom routine.** If you suspect a problem like this, have students tell their bedtimes, their "fall asleep" times, and what they ate for breakfast as a writing or retelling assignment. Repeat this exercise for a couple of weeks so that you get a good picture of how each student is starting his day. You can also send home the Home Routine Journal Page (page 69) as a writing or drawing assignment to help you get a better idea of students' routines.

- **Although unusual, it is possible for students to have disabilities that prevent them from hearing instructions or retaining the information.** If a student has particular difficulties with recalling routines, the student may have an auditory processing disorder, hearing loss, or even a dysfunctional short-term memory.

Routine Teacher

Student's Name: _____ Date: _____
Read the steps in the new routine. Draw a picture of each part of the routine.

STEP 1: Arrive at school

STEP 2: Hang up my coat

STEP 3: Put lunch box on shelf

STEP 4: Move name tag
I AM AT SCHOOL
Max

STEP 5: Sit in my seat

STEP 6: Start my seatwork

KE-804096 © Key Education   -68-   Teaching Tips for Challenging Behaviors

Routine Teacher

Student's Name: _____ **Date:** _____

Directions: Read the steps in the new routine. Draw a picture of each part of the routine.

STEP 1: _____	STEP 2: _____
STEP 3: _____	STEP 4: _____
STEP 5: _____	STEP 6: _____

Home Routine Journal Page

Student's Name: _____ **Date:** _____

Directions: Read the questions about what you do at home. Write your answers on the lines. If you need help, ask a family member.

Draw hands on the clocks to answer the questions.

1. What time did you get up today?

2. What time do you usually get up?

Draw your answers for these questions. Label your drawing.

3. What did you have for breakfast?

4. What is your favorite thing to have for dinner?

Write answers to these questions.

5. What things do you do every night to get ready for bed? _____

_____

_____

6. Do you have any jobs to do around the house? What are they? _____

_____

_____

Disorganization

Disorganization is not a huge issue for preschoolers, since most of them have their belongings and schedules organized by parents and teachers. In elementary school, disorganization can be a huge problem. Students go from forgetting show-and-tell items to forgetting to turn in school projects or study for tests. Disorganized students always seem to be searching for missing work that they will swear to you that they did. Unfortunately, they often did do it, then lost it. Procrastination, a separate but related issue, can result from students losing project guidelines, forgetting to write down dates, or being to overwhelmed to make a schedule and follow it. There is no worse feeling for many than being unprepared, and it causes plenty of stress for students.

Helping a disorganized student means being organized yourself. Everything in your classroom should have a home, and that home should be clearly labeled. Your assignments should be clear with definite due dates. And, the system you use to transfer information back and forth between parents and your classroom should be easy to follow, since often you will be training parents to be more organized, as well. Below are some tricks for helping students stay on the ball, and keep their parents there, too.

Indicators of Disorganization
- ❖ Personal areas within the classroom like backpacks, desks, or cubbies are messy.
- ❖ Papers are rarely discarded.
- ❖ Homework is sloppy; handwriting far exceeds space given.
- ❖ Appearance and other personal habits, like eating habits, may be messy.
- ❖ Tries to carry everything in hands instead of in a backpack or book bag.
- ❖ Frequently forgets homework or show-and-tell.
- ❖ Cannot clean up; is overwhelmed when it is time to put away toys or supplies.
- ❖ May be easily sidetracked as a result of an attention problem.
- ❖ May have trouble repeating directions back to you, even for simple tasks.
- ❖ Loses supplies, permission slip, and homework.
- ❖ Is generally forgetful.

Tricks and Tips for Helping Students Become More Organized

- ❖ **Walk around your room with an "eye for clutter."** If you find any cluttered areas, chances are, students notice those, too. Rework those areas to make them more accessible so students can help you keep them organized.

- ❖ **When possible, use picture labels to identify proper storage places for classroom supplies.** Even older students will appreciate visual help.

- ❖ **At the beginning of the school year, or more often if some students need it, have a review about how to store materials.** Show students how to put work in folders or notebooks. Review rules about when materials need to go home and when thing can be recycled.

- ❖ **Take a bathroom break before clean-up time** if students tend to use bathroom breaks as an excuse not to help out.

- ❖ **When you have clean-up time, give specific tasks that relate to what students played with.** For example, tell the student who got out all of the blocks to re-stack the blocks on the shelves. This may lead them to be less messy in the first place.

- ❖ **Verbally remind students to stay on task** by saying, "Anna, you are supposed to be putting the doll clothes back in the bin." Be sure to name both the object and the place it belongs.

- ❖ **Consider using timers for students who are resistant about cleaning up.** It is much harder to argue with a timer.

- ❖ **Complete clean-up.** Make sure students complete clean-up before moving to another activity.

- ❖ **During transition times,** verbally go over what students need for their next task so that they have time to get out materials.

- ❖ **Keep a consistent classroom routine** so students have a chance to organize their materials ahead of time.

- ❖ **When you do change the routine,** give plenty of warnings before transitioning to a new activity, so students have time to gather or put away homework and materials.

- ❖ **Set aside time in the morning and at the end of the day to go over assignments.** Use additional morning time to help students find their materials for the day, and afternoon time to review what they need to take home and return the following day.

- ❖ **When you have calendar time in the morning, review any upcoming assignment dates.** Let older students double-check due dates and event dates, and write them on copies of the Assignment Calendar page (page 72) at least once per week. If your students are too young to fill out the calendar themselves, fill out one for them and make copies.

- ❖ **Make sure you clearly define your expectations for what students should remember to bring in every day,** such as rain jacket or coat, lunch or money, homework, school books, materials, and assignments. After you review this, fill out the Do You Have Your_____? checklist (page 73). Copy it and send it home for parents to post in a prominent place, like on the back of the front door, where students will see it before they leave.

- ❖ **Help parents remember assignments and events so their young children are not penalized for parental disorganization.** Communicate with parents in several different ways, like e-mail, weekly newsletters, notes home, and more. Once you decide how you will communicate and how often, let parents know this information. If you are consistent, they will know where to look. (If parents are new to the school, this is especially important.)

- ❖ **Share your organizational system with parents so they can offer support from home.** For example, if homework comes home every Tuesday, or if show-and-tell happens every Friday, let parents know so that they can help students remember.

- ❖ **Clearly mark what work needs to return to school and what work can stay at home.** You can color code or stamp homework that needs to return.

- ❖ **Keep in mind that disorganization may be a symptom of situations** such as many children to keep up with, lots of activities, parents in separate households, family illness, or even very busy careers. The more support you can offer with organization, the easier things will be for your students.

Calendar Month:

Student's Name:

Sunday	Monday	Tuesday	Wednesday	Thursday	Friday	Saturday

Write the name of the month on the line. Write the numbers for the dates in the top, right hand corner of each square. Your teacher will tell you what due dates, field trips, and other events to add.

Do You Have Your...?

Fill in the blanks with things students should bring to school each day. Give a copy to each student to take home. Instruct parents to post this paper where their children will see it every day on their way out of the house. You can also use this at school for things students should take home every night.

Student's Name: _____

Date: _____

Do You Have Your:

☐ _____

☐ _____

☐ _____

☐ _____

☐ _____

☐ _____

Do You Have Your...?

Fill in the blanks with things students should bring to school each day. Give a copy to each student to take home. Instruct parents to post this paper where their children will see it every day on their way out of the house. You can also use this at school for things students should take home every night.

Student's Name: _____

Date: _____

Do You Have Your:

☐ _____

☐ _____

☐ _____

☐ _____

☐ _____

☐ _____

Chapter 6
Social and Emotional Development

❖ poor conversational skills ❖

❖ excessive or inappropriate talking ❖

❖ inappropriate physical contact and lack of respect for personal space ❖

❖ lack of personal care and hygiene ❖

❖ aggression and anger ❖ bullying v extreme shyness ❖

❖ immaturity ❖ excessive crying and sadness ❖ lying ❖

❖ inability to build friendships ❖ abuse-responsive behaviors ❖

❖ unresponsive to consequences ❖

One of the most important things students need to learn is social skills. Although it is not always an official part of curriculum, few things make school harder for students then having a tough time with their peers. There are all kinds of reasons students have a hard time getting along. Some do not know how to talk to friends. Some are extremely shy, or extremely aggressive. Some are just naturally loners.

It can be painful to watch children who are unsure of themselves socially. Teachers can help by observing, offering advice, and building in opportunities for social play. Playing, especially pretending, helps students learn to negotiate and compromise. They can try out different kinds of conversation as they imitate adults or favorite characters. And, students learn that there are great rewards to being kind and helpful while negotiating play. They make friends that way!

Poor social skills and lagging emotional development may have underlying causes. It is important to remember that a lot of "labels" fall under this umbrella. Autism spectrum disorders, ADHD, depression and personality disorders, and abuse or trauma can seriously affect how students navigate social situations. Although great strides are being made with early diagnoses, it can be very hard to definitively diagnose social and emotional problems in preschool. As students move into elementary school, the issues become more apparent. Be cautious; document your observations meticulously, and do not approach parents directly about any issues that might require diagnoses. Instead, get your director or principal involved, and make sure you leave diagnoses to professionals who have experience with the issues involved and with talking to parents.

Poor Conversational Skills

Students can usually get by with poor conversational skills while they are very young. As long as they can laugh with friends and understand how to share, words are not so important. From about age four or five, conversational skills become very important. Play becomes more complex and requires words. Students are expected to talk in groups as part of their class work. Teachers start calling on students for answers. A student who cannot participate will have a difficult time, especially in elementary school when participation becomes part of a grade.

There are many reasons students have poor conversational skills. Their speech may be unclear enough to prevent others from understanding them. They may not recognize how to give and take in a conversation. They may answer questions with irrelevant information, or not answer at all. Some students have few chances to practice conversation at home, or their parents may do the talking for them. Some may simply fail to pick up social cues like personal space, appropriate volume, body language, or turn taking.

The best way to help these students is to make sure they get plenty of practice. Play dates, role-playing, and ideas for how parents can engage students in conversations at home can help students learn to talk to each other. Spending one-on-one time with good listeners is the best way to bring out a student's desire to talk to others.

Indicators of Poor Conversational Skills
❖ Fails to connect with classmates because speech is not understandable. (See the section on Limited Speech (Clarity) on page 37.)
❖ Stands too close to others and talks in their faces.
❖ Stands across the room and shouts.
❖ Looks at the floor or makes no eye contact.
❖ Gives off unfriendly signals like a grouchy tone or eye-rolling. (This is the "prickly" student.)
❖ When spoken to, responds with a blank look or ignores the speaker entirely.
❖ Cannot initiate conversations.
❖ Has trouble holding other students' attention. (This is the student who runs after his friends yelling, "Guys, guys! Hey guys!" When they finally respond, the yeller often has nothing to say or says something silly.)
❖ Gives limited responses—yes, no, uh-uh, etc.

Tricks and Tips for Addressing Poor Conversational Skills

❖ **First and foremost, involve these students in as many conversations as possible.** Give them opportunities to chat with you, their friends, and other teachers. Practice can lead to real improvement.

❖ **Have students bring show-and-tell to class.** After a student describes her item, let classmates ask questions for the student to answer. You may need to prompt them to give detailed answers.

❖ **After sharing a book, ask the student to retell the story.** This is a difficult skill but it helps them work on maintaining a train of thought while talking.

❖ **Lack of eye contact can be cultural.** Many Americans, Canadians, and Europeans value eye contact, while other cultures view it as too personal or as a challenge. If a student is looking at his feet, it may be a sign of respect in his culture. Older students will understand that eye contact is expected if you explain it, but making any prolonged eye contact may be intimidating for younger students.

❖ **Remember that personal space can be cultural, as well.** Some students have been raised to stand very close to others. A student from another country may simply need a gentle hint that classmates prefer talking a little farther apart than she is used to. Let her know that if a classmate backs up just a little as they are talking, she should stand her ground instead of following, but should continue the conversation.

❖ **To demonstrate appropriate personal space,** tape boxes on the floor and have students stand in them to talk.

❖ **A trick that encourages eye contact is to ask students to tell you what color your eyes are when you start a conversation**—they have to look in your eyes to tell you.

❖ **Let students take turns talking to each other while you record them.** Play back their conversations and ask what they notice. Could they understand themselves? Did both students get a chance to talk? Talk with them about things they notice, like when they pause, when their voices get louder or softer, when they ask good questions, and when they give good answers. Find a compliment for every student.

❖ **If you teach preschool or have centers, provide items that encourage conversational role-playing,** like old cell phones, walkie-talkies, or even a drive-through restaurant setup.

❖ **Parents often use shyness as a justification for their children having poor conversational skills.** Better conversational skills can be a tool for students to overcome shyness, so ask that parents encourage their children to speak when spoken to.

❖ **Good listeners invite good conversation.** Practice asking questions, and show students how to stop and listen to their classmates' answers.

❖ **Try to break students of the habit of saying, "Huh?" "What?"** Encourage them to listen for their names, and be sure to call their names before speaking to them. Give them time to look at you before you start talking.

❖ **Use the What Should You Say? reproducible (page 77)** to gauge students' ideas of how conversations should work. Ask the questions in a whole-class setting and then talk about their answers.

❖ **Set an expectation in your classroom for students to respond to each other.** When a student keeps calling a classmate's name trying to get a response, it is fine to sometimes stop action in the classroom and wait for the classmate to respond. Explain that

when you or a classmate addresses someone, it is good manners to stop an activity, look the person in the eye, and answer them. (Make sure you use this behavior with students, too!)

❖ **Children need to learn how to take turns during conversations, make eye contact, wait an appropriate time for responses, and ask good questions.** Sit down with your assistant or a parent volunteer and let students watch you talk to each other. Then, pair students with partners. Let them choose a prompt from the Let's Have a Chat reproducible (page 78). Then, let students talk to each other about the prompt like you and the other adult. (If their conversation wanders, do not worry, as long as it continues.)

❖ **Role-playing can be funny and eye opening when the teacher does it.** Role-play poor conversational skills while talking to your students. For example, get too close, ask tons of questions without waiting for answers, interrupt, look at the floor, etc. After each scenario, ask students what you are doing that is funny (because they will probably be laughing at you). Be sure to include many different behaviors so that one student with poor conversational skills does not feel singled out. Next, model good conversational skills, like making eye contact and being a good listener.

❖ **Students with characteristics or diagnoses of autism, ADHD, or auditory processing disorders often have difficulty in conversations with other students.** All of these tips will be helpful for these students. But, if you suspect any of these disorders, especially autism spectrum, you may need to be more literally instructive with that student than with classmates. Students with autism have an especially hard time picking up on subtle social cues like body language. While their classmates may laugh at you when you move too close to talk, or when you look at the floor, a student with autism may have no idea what is funny, so try to explain the behavior, and model correct behavior so the student with autism can emulate it.

What Should You Say?

Name: _____ Date: _____

Ask students these questions, then talk about their answers. Older students can circle their own answers.

1. When someone asks, "How are you," you should say:
- A. Nothing
- B. Pictures
- C. Fine, thank you
- D. What?

2. If you need to talk to someone who is on the other side of the playground, you should:
- A. Yell his name until he hears you
- B. Throw things at him until he notices
- C. Walk over to talk to him
- D. Give up

3. When you talk to someone, you should stand:
- A. About an arm's length away
- B. Nose to nose
- C. Back to back
- D. On their foot

4. Which one of these is a good question to ask a new person?
- A. "Where are you going?"
- B. "What is your name?"
- C. "How high can you jump?"
- D. "Do you like me?"

5. When someone is talking to you, you should:
- A. Look at the ceiling
- B. Whistle or hum
- C. Listen and look at them.
- D. Run away.

6. Your friend says, "I like the book we read in class today." A nice thing to say back would be:
- A. "I didn't. It was awful!"
- B. "Hey, it's raining."
- C. "What was your favorite part?"
- D. "I really like math."

7. When you are talking with a group of friends, you should NOT:
- A. Interrupt
- B. Look at the floor
- C. Talk very loudly to be heard
- D. All of the above

8. Your sister just won her first soccer trophy. You should tell her:
- A. "I have THREE soccer trophies."
- B. "So?"
- C. Nothing
- D. "Good job! Where are you going to put it?"

9. Mrs. Brown, your neighbor, tells you she is getting a new puppy. A good thing to say might be:
- A. "What kind of puppy is it?
- B. "I just like cats."
- C. "My mom does not like pets."
- D. "I don't know."

10. Your dad says, "I had a rough day at work!" You could say:
- A. "Can we go out for pizza?"
- B. "Did you bring me a present?"
- C. "I am sorry you had a bad day."
- D. "My brother broke a glass. Is he in trouble?"

Let's Have a Chat

Name: _____ **Date:** _____

Directions: Sit with a friend. Take turns asking each other questions from this page. Ask your own questions to find out more about your classmate's friends.

1. Do you have any brothers or sisters? What are their names? Do you play with them?

2. What is your middle name? If you could pick a different name for yourself, what would it be?

3. What is your favorite thing about school? Why? Tell me about your least favorite thing.

4. Would you rather read, play video games, or play a sport? Which one would be hardest to give up?

5. What do you want to be when you grow up? What do you have to do to get that kind of job?

6. If you could have anything you want for dinner and dessert tonight, what would you pick?

7. What color is your room? If you could paint it any color, which one would you choose and why?

8. Which holiday is your favorite? Why? Do you have a least favorite?

9. What is the best thing we do at school every day? If you were the teacher, what would you change?

10. If you had $100 to spend on anything you wanted, what would you buy, and why?

Excessive or Inappropriate Talking

Some students never stop talking. From the moment they arrive at school, you and their classmates are treated to a nonstop narrative. Even when you ask them to stop talking, they cannot stay quiet for long. Excessive talking is one of the most commonly corrected behaviors in elementary school. It is great fun to talk, but the sooner students learn when it is not appropriate to chatter away, the easier their lives will be.

There are also students who may not talk constantly, but you certainly remember what they say: "Mrs. Welch, look at that boy picking his nose!" "Gary smells bad today!" "My mom says that I have the nicest clothes in my class." Comments like these are never hard to come by with students who have not learned to think before they speak. It can be difficult to teach them the fine line between honesty and hurting people's feelings. For example, if you tell your student that it is not nice to say that Gary smells, the response is likely to be, "But he does!" Yes, well, maybe he does, but we do not all need to hear about it. Poor Gary.

Once some students really come into their own with conversation, it is time to teach them appropriate timing and appropriate comments. Every teacher of young students has at least one story of a student who talks constantly, or of a bombshell that was dropped in class, often at the expense of another student or to the embarrassment of parents. While these stories may be funny or cute to you, they are neither if a classmate is embarrassed or hurt, or a private family conversation is shared. Learning how not to talk or how not to make inappropriate comments means learning to recognize social cues, and these can be very hard to teach. Here are some ideas for teaching students when not to talk, and what not to say.

Indicators of Excessive or Inappropriate Talking

- ❖ **Misunderstands or ignores social cues for when it is appropriate not to talk. (Talks while teacher is talking, or during times when students are supposed to be working silently.)**
- ❖ **Talks constantly. (Talks to hear himself talk.)**
- ❖ **Talks over and interrupts other students.**
- ❖ **Makes noises.**
- ❖ **Laughs at or joins in disruptive behavior.**
- ❖ **Touches others while talking to make sure they are paying attention.**
- ❖ **Shouts at inappropriate times; lacks volume control.**
- ❖ **Constantly gets off topic during class discussions. (This is normal for preschool students since they are learning to make connections. Elementary-age students should be able to stick to the topic more easily.)**
- ❖ **Talks without thinking and does not understand that others' feelings may be hurt.**

Tricks and Tips for Addressing Excessive or Inappropriate Talking

- ❖ **Teach students nonverbal signals,** like putting a finger to your lips, turning off lights, or shaking your head, to tell them it is time to be quiet.

- ❖ **When a student is talking inappropriately, stop talking and look at her** until she notices you are waiting on her to be quiet.

- ❖ **Decorate a stick with ribbons and streamers. Explain that this is the talking stick,** and that only the person who is holding it is allowed to talk.

Use it in group settings, and hold it yourself when it is the teacher's turn. Then, let students make their own talking sticks by gathering sticks from outside, painting them, and decorating them. Send the sticks home for families to use.

- ❖ **Older preschool and elementary students are ready to learn about raising hands when they want to talk.** When a student chimes in during a lesson without waiting to be called on, acknowledge the comment, then remind students to raise their hands.

- **Some students blurt out comments because they like the laughter that follows.** If you have a class clown, set the tone by ignoring the comments, but praise her when she raises her hand and responds appropriately.

- **If students constantly interrupt without raising their hands, bring in a pair of earmuffs.** When you wear them, tell students you cannot hear anything. You can only answer questions if you see them raise their hands. Then, pretend you cannot hear a word. They will start raising their hands soon enough. Do not forget to lift your earmuffs to listen to them or you will give away your secret.

- **Be patient with your talkers.** Often, their talking is more about their needs than it is about being disrespectful or disruptive. Some of these students are struggling to be more mature or to contribute, while others are simply "wired" to be chatty. Students who talk constantly or try to draw attention to themselves with loud talking may actually be craving attention. Try spending a little one-on-one time with these students to give them some extra attention. Also, talk to parents about the need for more interaction at home, and more play dates, too.

- **Some students are naturally more extroverted and need interaction in order to do their best work or to concentrate.** This goes against the quiet behavior that is usually rewarded in school. Try playing quiet music to help these students focus.

- **Empathy is a skill that some students must learn.** When a student says something hurtful, talk with him about why that hurt his friend's feelings. Make sure he offers a sincere apology. To further teach empathy, have students complete the Kind Things worksheet (page 81).

- **Explain the difference between telling a lie and saying something in a way that is not hurtful.** It never hurts to teach the old saying, "If you can't say anything nice, don't say anything at all." Reviewing what that means can help students stop and think before they speak.

- **Sometimes, students repeat things they hear from their parents when the parents think their children are not listening.** If necessary, have a conversation with parents about any information you think parents would not wish to have repeated. In class, explain the term, "family business," so that students understand that some things that happen at home need to stay at home. (Of course, if it seems that a child is being hurt or neglected at home you should encourage them to confide in an adult immediately.)

- **Ask the most disruptive student, "What do you think?" when you catch him talking.** After he gets put on the spot a few times, he is likely to quiet down unless he wants to get called on.

- **Imagining what other people are saying can help students think about appropriate give-and-take in conversations.** Let students fill in the speech bubbles on the What Are They Saying? reproducible (page 82). Let students compare their notes.

- **Remember that talking is not always a bad thing.** Part of a teacher's job is to get students to contribute, to share what they are learning, and to make suggestions and give answers. Try to channel their talking into lively class discussions.

Kind Things

Student's Name: _____ **Date:** _____

Directions: Make a list of kind things you could say to your friend. Sometime during the day, say one of these things to a friend. Draw a picture of you and the friend you were kind to. How does it feel to say kind things? How does it feel to hear them?

_____

_____

_____

_____

_____

_____

What Are They Saying?

Student's Name: _____ **Date:** _____

Directions: These students are talking about something they learned. What do you think they are saying? Write a sentence for each student. Draw a number next to each student to show who speaks first, second, third, and fourth.

Inappropriate Physical Contact or Lack of Respect for Personal Space

When a toddler bites or hits a classmate who snatched a toy away, or tries to kiss a teacher, this is normal behavior for the age group. Most students grow out of making impulsive contact as they develop self-control. However, students may use physical contact as a substitute for words long past the time when that is acceptable. It can take many different forms, too, from pinching someone who breaks in line, to wrestling a friend to the ground in a bear hug. At some point, students need to learn to keep their hands to themselves.

More difficult to eradicate are the less cut-and-dried behaviors that cause problems. Adults laugh at the phrase, "close talker," but students who do not understand body language and personal space may get right in their classmates' faces and make them uncomfortable. It is hard to explain how close is too close. Similarly, some students are very interested at an early age in exploring their own bodies and those of their classmates. It can be uncomfortable to discuss those behaviors, and also abstract, since some touching is fine and some is not, so read ahead to get ideas for where to draw the line and how to do it tactfully.

Indicators of Inappropriate Physical Contact
- ❖ Cannot keep hands to themselves; poking, pinching, patting, pulling hair, and touching are frequent.
- ❖ Hits, pushes, or bites instead of using words to express feelings.
- ❖ Kisses and hugs other classmates whether they want her to or not.
- ❖ Gets too close to others when talking to them.
- ❖ Initiates any kind of contact (with self or with classmates) that makes others uncomfortable.

Tricks and Tips for Limiting Inappropriate Physical Contact

- ❖ **Make your rules clear.** Explain that high fives, fist bumps, and holding hands are fine at school. Other touching is not fine, because it can bother classmates.

- ❖ **Carefully monitor the lunchroom, bathroom, playground, and field trips,** since there are plenty of touching opportunities there, when students are more loosely supervised.

- ❖ **Explain that kissing spreads germs and students should save kissing for home.**

- ❖ **If you have a student who constantly pokes and prods others,** group that student with two confident classmates who are likely to discourage this behavior on their own.

- ❖ **Role-play the phrase, "Hands to yourself."** Use a stuffed animal with long arms, such as a monkey or octopus. Demonstrate what it means to keep one's hands to oneself, and show the animal alternately bothering another stuffed animal and keeping its hands to itself.

- ❖ **If you have a student who cannot stop touching his seat mate,** pull his desk a few inches away from the other student so that the temptation is out of reach.

- ❖ **Hide the word *hands* in sentences to call attention to touching.** For example, if Jill is playing with Mara's hair during a counting lesson, say something like, "Now we are going to skip count *Hands Jill* by fives."

- ❖ **Let each student color and cut out a Paper Hand (page 85).** Collect the hands. When you see a student picking or poking, walk over and give that student a paper hand. As you see other students fail to keep their hands to themselves, give a paper hand to other students. At the end of the day, give a small reward to students who do not have a hand, like extra stickers or being the first to line up and leave the classroom.

❖ **If a student seems unable to control his hands, define the space more clearly.** Let the student work in a tabletop carrel, or sit on a carpet square or in a hoop or taped-off space. Define table spaces with place mats.

❖ **Provide other tactile experiences to distract the student from touching others.** A small textured ball or soft piece of fabric may help the student keep her hands appropriately occupied.

❖ **Tape an index card to a student's desk.** Each time you see him using his hands inappropriately, ask him to write a tally mark on his card. Look at each day's card and reward him if there is any progress.

❖ **Some students cannot keep their hands out of their pants.** If you notice children with their hands in their underwear, make them wash their hands. They will get tired of washing their hands so often and eventually break the habit. (This also applies for students who pick their noses or ears, or put their hands in their mouths to bite fingernails.)

❖ **Speak with parents about appropriate clothing.** Parents love to send their girls to school in dresses, but ask that shorts or tights be worn under the dress. Boys should wear fitted underwear under athletic shorts.

❖ **For students who hit or use their hands to hurt others, be careful not to reward their behavior with too much attention.** Remove them to a time out area, but spend the majority of your time making sure the classmate who was hit is not hurt, and returning to the lesson.

❖ **Students who realize that hitting hurts and makes friends sad are less likely to keep doing it and are showing signs that they are developing empathy.** Show the What Can Hands Do? reproducible (page 86) and talk about how the students in each drawing must feel. Older students can choose a drawing and write what they think is happening, telling how hands are being used.

Paper Hand

Student's Name: _____ **Date:** _____

Directions: Color the paper hand. Write your name on the back, then cut out the hand.
Give it to your teacher.

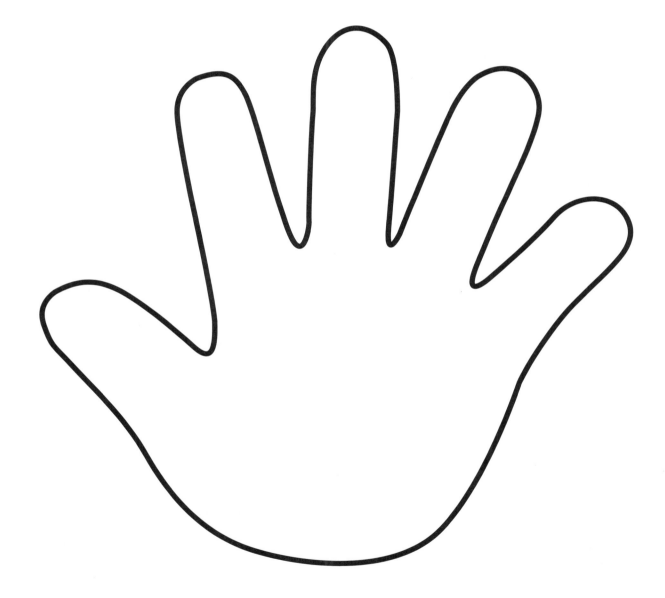

What Can Hands Do?

Student's Name: _____ **Date:** _____

Directions: Look at the scene in each box. Tell what is happening.   How do the students feel?
Should these students do things differently?

Lack of Personal Care and Hygiene

Every family has a different standard for hygiene, and students reflect those values as they come to school. Poor hygiene can be a distraction for the student and others, and can even result in the student's being left out or bullied. For these reasons, it can become necessary to help the student with hygiene habits, and even to address the issue with parents. Hygiene is a touchy subject. A lack of good hygiene can be related to socioeconomic status in cases where parents are financially unable to provide good hygiene tools for their children, or who have not learned good hygiene practices themselves. If you do anything to help a student practice better hygiene, do so with great sensitivity and tact, since it can be hurtful to both the student and his family. Definitely ask your principal or director to assist with the discussion; it is appropriate protocol and a third party can help diffuse a tense situation.

Indicators of Lack of Personal Care and Hygiene

❖ Has visible dirt or noticeable smell, either on skin or clothing.
❖ Has unbrushed hair or teeth.
❖ Wears worn clothing (to the extent that clothing is falling apart).
❖ Has poor hygiene habits: nose picking, dislike of hand washing, poor toileting habits.
❖ Brings a dirty lunch box to school.
❖ Desk is overflowing with papers, snack wrappers, and other objects.
❖ Has lice. (Immediately take a student with lice to the nurse's office. Lice are very contagious and must be addressed by the school administration upon discovery.)

Tricks and Tips for Improving Personal Care and Hygiene

❖ **Keep hygiene supplies on hand in case of emergencies.** Store new toothbrushes, trial-size toothpaste, soap, hair accessories, small plastic combs, wipes, tissues, breath mints, child-approved mouthwash, and even extra clothing in a box in your classroom. (Students should never share personal care items, so make sure each item has one user by labeling them or throwing them out after use.) Make the items available to students who need them, but do so very discreetly.

❖ **If you need to help some students with their hygiene, try to do so first thing in the morning so that they can spend the rest of their day feeling a little cleaner.** Other students are more distracted as they are arriving, so they will be less likely to notice you helping that student.

❖ **Approach hygiene as a classroom health issue, and make it a part of your health curriculum.** As a class, practice brushing teeth, washing hands and faces, and combing and styling hair. Explain why each practice is important, and explain why all should be done at least twice per day.

❖ **You can teach hygiene skills to younger students as part of a larger self-help unit.** During this unit, you can also teach students how to tie shoes, button clothing, comb hair, buckle belts, and tuck in shirts.

❖ **Entice preschoolers to use good hygiene with center play.** Set up a barber shop/salon, dentist office, or play bathroom for dolls in your classroom. Help teach students rules of good hygiene as they play in the centers.

❖ **Send home the Healthy Hygiene Checklist (page 89)** to monitor students' use of good hygiene at home. (This is a good idea if several students have issues. It conveys the need for good hygiene to parents, too.)

❖ **Invite a doctor, nurse, or dentist to discuss good hygiene with your class.** Hopefully, the guest speaker will have some goodies to share with students, like antibacterial gel or toothbrushes and floss.

❖ **Always have tissues available for students who pick their noses.** It is less disruptive to take a box of tissues to the student who needs them than it is to call them down verbally.

❖ **Each time a student picks his nose, have him wash his hands.** The repeated interruption may help him break the habit.

❖ **Work out a nonverbal signal** to remind a student not to pick his nose or bite his nails.

❖ **Have a lunch box-washing day with students.** Immediately after lunch, fill up a tub or your sink with warm water and dish soap. Let each student take a turn washing her lunch box. Then, have students bring their lunch boxes outside during playground time. Spread out some beach towels and let students spread the lunch boxes on their beach towels to dry in the sun.

❖ **In some cases, you may need to decide whether poor hygiene crosses the line into actual neglect.** Use the Healthy Child Checklist (page 89) to help you decide whether you need to take steps to report possible neglect to your director or principal.

❖ **If you do determine that a student is suffering from neglect, involve your principal or preschool director immediately.** A supervisor will be able to follow the proper protocol to ensure follow-up with a related agency. Make sure you document dates and specific instances of signs of neglect; those reports can be very important in establishing grounds to investigate. (See page 119 for more about neglect.)

Healthy Hygiene Checklist

Student's Name:

_____

Date: _____

Check the box next to each thing that you did before school. Draw a picture of yourself doing one thing on the list:

☐ I brushed my teeth.

☐ I washed my face.

☐ I combed my hair.

☐ I washed my hands after I used the restroom.

☐ I put on clean clothes.

☐ I wiped my face after I ate breakfast.

Healthy Hygiene Checklist

Student's Name:

_____

Date: _____

Check the box next to each thing that you did before school. Draw a picture of yourself doing one thing on the list:

☐ I brushed my teeth.

☐ I washed my face.

☐ I combed my hair.

☐ I washed my hands after I used the restroom.

☐ I put on clean clothes.

☐ I wiped my face after I ate breakfast.

Hygiene Checklist

Student's Name: _____ **Date:** _____

Use this checklist to document instances when a student comes to school with poor hygiene. Check each of these statements that apply to a particular student. If you check more than three statements, discuss this checklist with your school principal or director. If necessary, you can summarize your observations on the Observation Summary Form (page 6).

The student is frequently dirty. *(List recent dates and observations.)*

The student's body/clothing/breath frequently has a bad odor. *(List recent dates and observations.)*

The student's clothing is dirty, torn, ill-fitting, or inappropriate for the weather.
(List recent dates and observations.)

The student frequently comes to school sick. *(List recent dates and observations.)*

The student has excessive absences. *(List recent dates and observations.)*

The student often has a dirty lunch box, an inadequate lunch, or no lunch money.
(List recent dates and observations.)

Aggression and Anger

Every teacher encounters at least one student who acts out in anger. Anger can be directed at almost anyone or anything, including classmates, teachers, and even objects. Some students quickly learn to control situations through anger. In preschool, angry outbursts are to be expected until students get old enough to use their words and gain self-control. But in late preschool and early elementary school, this behavior cannot be tolerated. An angry, aggressive student can make the classroom environment tense and difficult. Repeated outbursts of anger are frightening, disruptive, and puts students at risk.

Anger can be a red flag for all kinds of situations that need to be addressed. An angry student may need to be evaluated by a guidance counselor. A counselor can follow procedures to make sure that the student is not being abused at home. (See page 119 for more information about abuse.) A counselor can also help the student find more appropriate ways to manage anger. If the suggestions here do not work for your angry student, seek help from a guidance counselor.

Indicators of Aggression and Anger

- ❖ **Is rude to authority figures.**
- ❖ **Overreacts to any kind of criticism or discipline (shouting, kicking toys).**
- ❖ **Puts excessive stress on competition and winning and losing.**
- ❖ **Frequently loses temper and gets overwhelmed when things do not go his way.**
- ❖ **Hits or otherwise hurts classmates, either on purpose or "accidentally."**
- ❖ **Anger is so intense that it causes crying or headaches.**
- ❖ **Uses foul language.**
- ❖ **Shouts.**
- ❖ **Withdraws or sulks after losing a confrontation or in reaction to discipline.**

Tricks and Tips for Improving Aggression and Anger

❖ **Be patient with young preschoolers who use their hands (or teeth) instead of words to react to something they do not like.** Often, they are too frustrated to get any words out and react in the only way they know how. By age three of four, however, students are ready to start putting that behavior behind them.

❖ **Redirection is often more effective than punishment for very young students.** Unless someone is hurt and there is a need for an apology, try to distract an angry student with another center, with being a helper, or with the fact that it is time for snack or a trip to the playground.

❖ **Do not let students' anger surprise you, even if a normally docile student suddenly starts to lash out.** Anger is a normal part of development, and students who learn to recognize and then act on their anger are old enough to learn about the need to control it.

❖ **Some young students throw things or destroy things when they get angry.** If a student throws something, put that object in "time out" until it can behave. The object should be out of reach, but still visible, so the student cannot play with it but is reminded of the behavior.

❖ **Establish two quiet areas in your preschool classroom.** One should be a time-out area, where students are sent for misbehaving for a length of time designated by the teacher. The other should just be a quiet area. Let angry students sit in the quiet area when they are angry and need time to control themselves. Do not use this area as a punishment; offer it as an escape—a chance to back down gracefully. In the quiet area, students should self-determine when they are ready to calm down and rejoin the class.

- **Watch for students who learn to push each other's buttons.** Some students rub each other the wrong way, and seating them at different tables or putting them at opposite ends of the circle is often the easiest solution.

- **If an elementary-age student is acting out in class, diffuse the situation quickly.** If you cannot get the situation under control, removing the student from the classroom is a better solution than rewarding angry behavior with attention by stopping class to have a confrontation.

- **If a student destroys something, display the broken object** for a while as a reminder of what happens when a student cannot control her temper. Do not be too quick to replace the object—if you replace it at all.

- **It is never too early to develop empathy.** Make sure the angry student apologizes for the disruption. Explain how his outburst kept others from learning or enjoying themselves, but do not dwell on this for too long of a time. It is necessary only that the student knows what his behavior did to the rest of the class.

- **Once students learn to count or recite the alphabet, teach them to count to ten or say the alphabet when they feel themselves getting angry.** Not only does this give them time to cool down, it also requires that they concentrate hard if counting or saying letters is a recently-learned skill, and that can diffuse the situation.

- **If a preschool student pouts or withdraws in anger, refrain from coaxing him back into an activity.** Let the student withdraw and do not invite him back into the action, because this gives him the control to say, "No, I will not come over to circle time." Try to do the same for tantrums, unless they are truly too disruptive for other activities to continue.

- **If a student seems angrier than normal, ask parents to let you know of any family situations that might be causing the anger.** Keep parents up-to-date with any behavior modifications you put in place.

- **Use a reward system to help students learn self-control.** Give each student a copy of the Caught Being Good sticker sheet (page 93). Each time a day passes and a student shows self-control, give him a sticker for the day. Let the student visit the toy box when the sheet is full.

- **Use reverse psychology with a reward system.** Laminate the Caught Being Good sticker sheet (page 93) for each student. Cover the spaces on the laminated sheets with vinyl stickers (clings). If a student gets angry and acts out, have her remove a cling from the sheet. Be sure to allow extra chances to refill the sheet throughout the day. A student with a full sheet gets a prize!

- **Uncontrollable anger in a student can indicate that something is bothering him.** Offer a chance for students to communicate about the Things that Make Me Angry reproducible (page 94). After students circle their responses, they can write about something that makes them angry—and maybe give you a clue about how to help them control their anger.

- **If a student really cannot control herself, let her play alone.** Cast this as letting her be in charge of an entire center or set of manipulatives.

- **Finally, check your own anger at the door.** A teacher who gets angry easily is not doing much to teach students to control themselves. Plus, if you let your anger get the best of you in every stressful situation, it is much less effective each time.

Caught Being Good

Get caught being good. Fill up your sticker chart.

That Makes Me Angry!

Student's Name: _____ **Date:** _____

Circle the things that make you angry.

My friend hit me.	I lost a tooth.	My dad sent me to my room.
I had to sit in time out.	I tore my pants.	I got to have dessert after dinner.
I got a new shirt.	My game got rained out.	I saw a funny movie.
I dropped my cake on the floor.	My friends laughed at me.	I fell in the mud.
My job was to be line leader today.	My sister shared her candy.	I caught the ball.

Bullying

You may have heard that bullying is not what it used to be. The definition of bullying has been expanded to include exclusion and spreading rumors. These actions can be just as harmful as physical actions. Think that girls do not bully each other? Watch a group on the playground telling one classmate, "I told everyone you're a loser. You can't play with us." Additionally, with technology available to many students who are not ready for it, e-mails, social networks, and texts provide efficient ways for students to bully each other.

Stopping the bully is a good solution, but this chapter also has ideas to help the student who is the frequent target of bullying. Some students are marked from an early age because of appearance, socioeconomic status, or because they seem vulnerable. A student who is a constant target will need lots of support and strategies for defending herself without escalating the situation.

Indicators of Bullying

For the Bully
- ❖ Attacks classmates.
- ❖ Classmates avoid playing with this student.
- ❖ Frequently "borrows" others' possessions.
- ❖ Tells other students what to do and how to do it; is overly controlling.
- ❖ Never takes blame for accidents that happen around her.
- ❖ Excludes certain classmates.
- ❖ Exhibits sneaky behavior; tells lies.
- ❖ Seems to have a "gang" of followers.

For the Target
- ❖ Cries frequently but will not say why.
- ❖ Avoids playing with a certain classmate or group of classmates.
- ❖ Seems to dread certain situations, like lunch or recess.
- ❖ Complains of being sick at the same time each day (to avoid a situation in which she is targeted).
- ❖ Frequently misses school.
- ❖ Seems fearful, sad, or angry.
- ❖ Starts bullying others.
- ❖ "Loses" lunch money or possessions.

Tricks and Tips for Eradicating Bullying

- ❖ **Know what is going on with your students.** This sounds simple, but it means watching and listening carefully on the playground, in the hallways and lunchroom, and listening at the bathroom door. Bullies can be sneaky; catching them in the act means that no one has the burden of feeling like a tattletale.

- ❖ **Expect bullies to deny bullying behavior or to blame others, in a "He ran into my fist," sort of way.** If this happens, repeat exactly what you saw and heard or what was reported to you.

- ❖ **When you confront a bully, remain calm to show you are in control.**

- ❖ **Document all instances of bullying, both physical and emotional.**

- ❖ **Parents may come to you if they have had trouble with bullying in the past.** If a parent confides that a child has been in trouble for bullying, make that parent part of your team. Discuss strategies and outcomes from the past. Ask that parent to coordinate rewards and punishments that translate from school to home.

- ❖ **Conference with parents about the student's home life.** Is there stress in the home? Is there a lot of competition? Do siblings get along? What is a normal day like? Some of the responses may provide clues to the source of bullying. A bully may just be trying to get some control when he does not have any at home.

- **Assign students in pairs that can support each other in reporting bullying.** This will spread control around when various students are assigned to be in charge of monitoring areas where you cannot follow, like the bathroom.

- **Give a bully a special responsibility that does not involve classmates,** like cleaning out art supplies, caring for the class pet, or cutting out letters for the bulletin board. This removes the bully from classmates (and gives them a break); plus it lets you connect with the bully in a new way.

- **If you pair or group students, stick closest to the group with a known bully in it.** If he is not given the chance to pick on others, he may find he enjoys interacting with them in a more positive way.

- **Empathy can reduce bullying.** Role-play bullying situations with students. Ask how they would feel if someone did that to them.

- **When role-playing, do not just focus on bullies and targets.** Students, and indeed most people, are unprepared for how to act when they are bystanders to bullying. Give classmates strategies, such as telling a teacher, taking the targeted student to another area, and telling the bully to stop the harmful behavior can help students learn how to react without ignoring the bullying, joining in, or putting themselves in danger.

- **Reward positive behavior as often as possible, but make it clear to the bully that you expect good behavior at all times,** not just when she thinks she will be rewarded. Use the You Did Something Great Today! certificate (page 97) to let the student know you are paying attention to her good behavior.

Being a Target of Bullying

- **From the beginning, monitor students who are likely targets:** students who are smaller or larger than average, who seem shy or physically weaker than others, who are socially awkward, who are somehow different from their peers, or who get upset easily. Keeping an eye on these students can lead you to the bullies.

- **Suffering in silence can be very damaging.** Encourage students to come to you in private with any problems. Provide a variety of ways for students to contact you—passing you a note in class, telling you a secret (in preschool), or spending time with you as a special helper, to give them access.

- **There is a fine line between fitting in and conforming.** Celebrate differences in your classroom, but also find commonalities. For example, chart eye and hair color to show that all students have one of three colors of eyes. Get students together to talk about their pets, or favorite sports. Conversely, celebrate one student's talent as an artist, or compliment a student on how hard he worked on a science project. Finding similarities and appreciating differences helps students be more real and familiar to each other.

- **Further appreciation for classmates by having each student fill out a Write Something Kind note (page 97)** to a fellow classmate. Assign classmates or have students draw names to avoid duplicates. Students who are not writing yet can dictate their answers, and you can read them to the class.

- **Role-playing can be helpful to students who are targets of bullying.** Teaching students to walk away, to tell someone, or to stand up for themselves without escalating the situation can help them in real situations.

- **"So?" is one of the best comebacks a targeted student can use in response to teasing.** It does not start the "am not/are too" debate, and it often leaves the bully without a snappy retort.

- **Shake up the dynamics in your classroom.** Seat students together who are not friends or enemies. Getting new students together can form new alliances and build confidence in a student who is getting picked on.

- **For younger students, suggest specific play dates to parents.** Making new friends can help students avoid students who are unkind to them.

- **Take breaks from competition in P. E. and on the playground.** Instead, do activities that stress teamwork.

- **In group work or even in center play, assign a role to each student so that everyone has to contribute equally.**

- **Finally, it is up to you to protect students in your classroom so that no one gets hurt.** Make sure you document all instances of bullying that go beyond a little teasing, and report every significant incident. Refer students who cannot be kind to a guidance counselor.

You Did Something Great Today!

Student's Name: _____

Date: _____

_____

- -

_____

_____

- -

_____

_____

- -

Write Something Kind

To My Friend: _____

Write a friend's name on the name line. Write something you like about that friend.
Sign your name at the bottom.

_____

- -

_____

_____

- -

_____

_____

- -

From: _____ **Date:** _____

Extreme Shyness

Shyness is a big reason that many parents are holding students, particularly girls, back an extra year before they enter kindergarten. A little shyness is not a bad thing; it shows caution, and quiet behavior is often rewarded in school. However, there is a difference between being quiet and shy. Some students simply think before they speak, but they have no problem making friends or making their needs known. When a student is too shy to ask for what she needs, to stand up for herself, or to make friends, then shyness becomes a problem.

Indicators of Extreme Shyness

❖ Appears uncomfortable in new situations, far beyond other students' levels of discomfort.
❖ Will not make eye contact.
❖ Allows parents to speak for him.
❖ Plays side-by-side with others, rather than engaging them (applies to older preschool and to elementary students).
❖ Is avoided by other students because she will not engage with them.
❖ Has poor social skills.
❖ Acts nervous and fidgety.
❖ Goes along with the crowd because it is easier.
❖ Does not participate in whole class or group activities.
❖ Does not like raising his hand or participating in show-and-tell.
❖ Talks too softly to be heard.

Tricks and Tips for Improving Extreme Shyness

❖ **First of all, be patient.** That shy student who stays in the book center all day may soon warm up to others. Everyone comes out of their shell at their own pace.

❖ **Encourage parents to help their child practice talking about his "show and tell" object or story.** Let parents know in advance when show-and-tell will be. Use the Show-and-Tell Practice page (page 43) for additional help.

❖ **If you meet a shy student whose parents have gotten in the habit of speaking for him, wait until they are finished,** then ask for the student to respond in his own words.

❖ **Encourage parents to stop using, "He's shy," as an excuse for their child's reluctance** to make eye contact and respond. Doing both of these are basic good manners.

❖ **All students, not just the shy ones, suffer when families do not have conversations.** Encourage parents to talk to their children often. Use the Dinner Table Talk worksheet (page 100) with parents to help them find topics of conversation with their children.

❖ **Sit by the door and greet students with, "Good morning!"** Wait until they look you in the eye and respond before letting them enter the classroom.

❖ **Give shy students jobs that require getting up in front of the class,** like line leader and calendar helper.

❖ **At the beginning of the school year, let shy students volunteer** (or avoid volunteering) to contribute to class discussions, then gradually draw them out by calling on them.

❖ **Shy students tend to nod or shake their heads.** Ask them to talk instead, saying, "I cannot hear your head. Please use your words."

❖ **Teach students the "stop, look, and listen" rule.** When you speak to a student, he should stop what he is doing, look at you, then answer. And, make sure you practice this when students try to get your attention, to set a good example.

- ❖ **Ask open-ended questions** that have sentence-length answers instead of asking questions with yes or no answers.

- ❖ **Have frequent discussions with shy students.** Because they are hard to get to know, they may feel they are not very interesting, so be interested in them. Ask about their pets, hobbies, artwork, favorite games and books, and more until you finally find a topic they like so much they are excited to tell you about it.

- ❖ **Pair a shy student with a gregarious, but calm classmate.** Often, talkative students are good at drawing shy students into conversations. If possible, assign the pair a special task, like taking care of a class pet, so they have a chance to get to know each other and have something to talk about.

- ❖ **Suggest play dates to parents.** Playing with a classmate will give a shy student valuable time out of his comfort zone, and can reinforce a budding friendship.

- ❖ **Shy students can get lost in the shuffle of a noisy classroom.** Arrange for some quiet activities each day. Self-selected reading, rest time, story time, and table work can all quiet students down, so alternate these activities with louder activities.

- ❖ **Laughter can break tension and make a shy student feel comfortable.** Read funny stories, watch a funny video, or tell a funny story about yourself. Once students start laughing together, they may be inclined to play better together.

- ❖ **Ice breaker games can help students get to know each other.** For example, play Secret Fact. Have each student write a secret fact about herself—something interesting that no one else knows—on a piece of paper. Collect the papers and read each one aloud. Let three volunteers guess whose secret fact you read. If no one guesses, that student should stand up to get her paper.

- ❖ **Another good ice breaker game is matching cards.** Prepare a set of matching cards. They can have the same color dots, the same shapes, opposite words, matching letters, etc. Make a pair

of matching cards for each set of students. Pass out the cards, then let students find the classmates with the matching cards. When each pair meets up, each of them has to tell something about himself to his classmate.

- ❖ **Let students take home copies of the What's Your Favorite? worksheet (page XX).** As you find out information about students, graph the information to show students how they compare. Information like ice cream preferences, number of siblings, number of pets, and other things that are not so obvious as hair color and eye color will be interesting for students to find out.

- ❖ **Have sharing time during story time or morning meeting time.** Let each student share something about himself or tell about something special he has done.

- ❖ **Take pictures of students doing things in the classroom.** Let each student shown in the picture retell what she was doing at the time. Hang the pictures in the classroom where students can see them.

Dinner Table Talk

Student's Name: _____ **Date:** _____

Directions: Take home this piece of paper. Read the sentences.
When you have a family dinner, talk about one of the sentences.

1. Tell about the nicest teacher you have ever had.

2. If you could drive any car in the world, what car would it be? Where would you drive it?

3. Name all of the states you have visited. Which was your favorite? Your least favorite? Tell why.

4. If you could build an awesome playground, what would it look like?

5. Would you rather have a pet monkey, a fish, a rabbit, a skunk, or a horse?

6. What is the strangest food you can imagine eating for dinner?

7. If you had a private island, would you want it to be a jungle, a desert, or very cold?

8. Tell about the scariest movie you have ever seen or the scariest dream you ever had.

9. What is your earliest memory?

10. What do you think makes a happy family?

What's Your Favorite?

Student's Name: _____ **Date:** _____

Answer the questions to tell about some of your favorite things. Draw a picture of one of your answers.

What's your favorite...

Ice cream flavor?	Season?	Vegetable?
Fruit?	Book?	Song?
Toy?	Sound?	Smell?

Immaturity

Some students just seem younger than their classmates. First children and only children are often subject to more solicitous, less fend-for-yourself parenting, since this is easier to do with one child. To this fact, add the vast age difference between younger and older students in a classroom (partly due to the fact that many parents now hold their students back from entering kindergarten), and you can have more than a year's difference in ages in your classroom.

While maturity differences should be expected with age differences, some students have a hard time acting age-appropriately. One strong reason parents and teachers hold students back is a lack of maturity. Immature behavior, like silliness, poor social skills, general lack of self-control, hitting or biting after age four, impulsiveness, and a tendency to be the class clown can hold students back from learning and making friends, especially in elementary school when young students prefer to emulate their older schoolmates. While no student should be expected to grow up too quickly, there are some tricks you can use to help students learn self-control and independence that is age-appropriate.

Indicators of Immaturity

❖ Lags behind in self-help skills. (For example, expects a teacher to blow her nose for her because her parents do it at home, or resists potty training long past age three.)
❖ Suffers separation anxiety, even when being left in familiar places, past age five.
❖ Very impulsive; often speaks or acts before thinking.
❖ Becomes excessively sad or upset at changes in routine or minor disappointments. Inflexible.
❖ Dreads new situations.
❖ Cannot play alone.
❖ Clingy.
❖ Needlessly destructive; dumps out bins or breaks toys for fun.
❖ Laughs too loudly or too long without really understanding what the joke is.
❖ Disrupts the class; is unable to be "ready to learn."
❖ Uses bathroom humor long after most students have grown out of it.
❖ Looks to friends for confirmation after exhibiting bad behavior.

Tricks and Tips for Improving Immaturity

❖ **Remember that all students mature at different rates.** A student's home life, gender, culture, birth order, and birth date relative to those of classmates' all influence how quickly he matures. Always look for progress.

❖ **Obviously, immaturity is more of an issue in readiness and elementary school because it can get in the way of learning as students get older.** Compare a student's behavior with that of peers who are closest in age to determine whether immaturity is a problem or the behavior is actually somewhat in line with others.

❖ **Students who are hungry, sick, or very tired are often unable to control themselves.** Check for these issues when you have repeated problems with immaturity. Sometimes all it takes to settle those students down is a conversation with parents about getting their child to bed an hour earlier or offering more time for breakfast.

❖ **If a student seems exceptionally clingy to parents, encourage them to be low-key about leaving their child.** A simple hug, kiss, and, "I will see you at three," are preferable to, "I will miss you so much!"

❖ **As you plan the classroom schedule, remember that every student needs time to be silly and goofy.** Build in time for recess every day, even when it seems impossible. The rewards of students who have relaxed and refocused outweigh any academic time you might lose.

❖ **Work with students on age-appropriate self-help skills to build confidence and show them the upside of maturity.** Let a student who needs to gain maturity complete the I Can Do It! worksheet (page 104). Let her check off skills as she learns them, and offer plenty of praise as she becomes more independent.

- ❖ **Part of being mature is doing one's own work.** Well-meaning parents are often unsure of how much help to give. After you have had a chance to determine where each student is in each subject area or skill set, send home a note outlining some goals for each student to work toward. Differentiate each note to fit each student, and offer suggestions for what help parents should give, if any.

- ❖ **Students who are immature often have not learned to look at themselves through others' eyes.** Demonstrate inappropriate laughing, being disruptive, or saying inappropriate things. Ask students to tell you what you are doing to disturb the class.

- ❖ **Help the student compare her behavior to others.** Say, "Do you see that your friends have stopped laughing? It is not funny any more, is it?"

- ❖ **Many young students are self-centered; they do not consider how their actions affect others.** When a student disrupts the class, explain that others have to wait until she gets control over herself, or stops making noise. Gently explain that she is keeping her friends from learning.

- ❖ **If a student seems truly unaware of how his behavior affects others, videotape the student and let him watch the tape privately.** Point out how certain behaviors make it hard for the class to work and listen.

- ❖ **Establish a "class norm" for good behavior. Let students follow the Happy and Sad Stick Directions (page 105).** Demonstrate appropriate behaviors and immature behaviors as if you are a student in your own classroom. When you start a new behavior, ask students to hold up their sticks to show whether they are happy or sad about your behavior. Emulate behaviors you see in your classroom but do not single out any one student.

- ❖ **Explain what it means to "think before you speak or act."** Have students tell what can happen when they blurt out silly comments or act without thinking first. They can hurt friends' feelings, spill a secret, hurt or embarrass someone, and get into trouble. This is a valuable and hard lesson to learn.

- ❖ **Have a ritual that signals when it is time to start paying attention.** For example, when you say, "1-2-3, hands in your lap and eyes on me!" students should stop what they are doing, sit still, and pay attention.

- ❖ **Agree on a signal to subtly tell a student that her behavior is inappropriate.** For example, when she laughs for too long of a time at a funny book, silently shake your head at her to have her check her behavior.

- ❖ **Since immaturity can be a way to get attention, reward good behavior with attention instead.** Use the Caught Being Good (page 93) from (previous chapter) to reward students who act appropriately each school day. When a student makes it through the day without being called down for acting up, let her put a sticker on her chart. When the chart is full, let the student have a special treat, such as a visit to the treasure box.

- ❖ **Whenever there is a break in the routine, such as a field trip, remind students ahead of time to practice self-control.** Have a class discussion about what behavior is expected. Ask questions like, "What do you do if you need to go to the bathroom?" or "How should we act when the tour guide is speaking?"

- ❖ **Immaturity multiplies when two silly students sit together.** Seat immature students next to more mature classmates. The mature student is less likely to react to his silly classmate, so immature outbursts go unrewarded with attention. Also, seat students who compete with or "one-up" each other apart, to keep things like hoarding supplies and playing the ever-popular "Am not/are too" game.

- ❖ **Occasionally, a student who causes disruption is under-challenged and bored.** Keep him busy with extra work, a chapter book to read between lessons, a classroom job, or a special project he can work on at his own pace. For a very young student, draw his name in block letters and have him color the letters when he is finished with assignments, or give him an envelope full of torn out Box Tops to cut out. Older students can draw a scene from a favorite book, or complete extra chapters of a book as they wait for the next assignment.

I Can Do It!

Student's Name: _____ **Date:** _____

Directions: When you learn to do something new, give yourself a sticker.
Add more new things on the lines.

_____ I can go to the restroom quietly.

_____ I can button or zip my jacket.

_____ I can open my lunch containers.

_____ I can tie my shoes.

_____ I can ask good questions.

_____ I can share with my friends.

_____ I can write my name.

_____ I can _____

_____ I can _____

_____ I can _____

_____ I can _____

_____ I can _____

_____ I can _____

Happy and Sad Stick Directions

Directions:

1. Get a craft stick from your teacher.

2. Cut out the happy face.

3. Cut out the sad face.

4. Put one circle on top of the other so that you can see the happy face on one side and the sad face on the other.

5. Tape the circles together at the top.

6. Put the craft stick between the circles.

7. Tape the circles to the craft stick.

Excessive Crying and Sadness

Crying is a reaction to strong feelings. Not being able to keep from crying is the ultimate sign of "losing your cool." Students cry when parents leave, when they want to control a situation or to get something; because they are sensitive; out of anger and frustration; or fear of a new situation. Or, they may have a reason to be sad: family illness, divorce, or death. Dealing with students' crying is as simple as offering comfort and distractions in preschool. In elementary school, students who cry often may be teased or targeted by classmates, so it is more important to help the student learn to deal with strong feelings without crying, when possible.

One other type of "sad" student is the student who is fascinated by death and dying. Perhaps there has been a recent death in the family, or they have heard about it at a religious service. It does not take much imagination to think about loved ones dying, or even their own deaths. This particular fear can require some special handling.

Some students suffer from childhood depression. Persistent crying and sadness can be a sign of depression, especially when combined with lethargy, withdrawal from friends, extreme sensitivity or anger, changes in behavior, loss of appetite, frequent complaints of headaches or stomachaches, and talk of running away or suicide. If a student acts sad for more than a short time or is unable to pinpoint what is making her sad, it may be time to talk to your principal, director, or school counselor and plan to meet with parents and recommend an evaluation.

Indicators of Excessive Crying and Sadness

❖ Clings to parents at school drop-off.
❖ Cries during stressful situations, like during group work or playground games.
❖ Bursts into tears when disciplined.
❖ Frustrates classmates by crying when she does not get her way.
❖ Seems sad, withdrawn, lethargic, or unable to participate.
❖ Has difficulty expressing himself appropriately, often resorting to tears instead of words.
❖ Arrives late for school (due to crying before coming to class).
❖ Frequently does not turn in homework; seems unmotivated.
❖ Asks repeated questions about death and dying, or fears death of self or family members.

Tricks and Tips for Improving Excessive Crying and Sadness

Crying Due to Separation

❖ **At drop-off, instruct parents to give a hug, make eye contact, say that they will return soon, and then leave without lingering.** Ask them not to say, "I'll miss you!" Children are sad if they think their parents are sad.

❖ **A young student may find comfort in a favorite blanket or stuffed animal.** Agree to store the object in the student's backpack, and not the student's cubbie, since leaving it at school will cause great stress at bedtime!

❖ **Redirection is magic.** Distract a sad student with a favorite toy, a good friend, a song, or silly behavior. Older students can lose themselves as you read aloud, visit the media center, or do a favorite classroom activity.

❖ **Expect longer adjustment periods for students who attend only a few days of school per week.** Students who follow the same routine each day are faster to adjust than students who are only in school a few days.

❖ **If a young student is inconsolable, arrange a staggered schedule.** Have the parent pick up the student after an hour for a few days. Gradually lengthen the time at school until she stays for the full day without crying.

Crying to Get Her Way

❖ **Ignoring tantrums will stop crying much faster than negotiating, pleading, or punishment.** It is hard to watch a disruptive tantrum, but worse to encourage the behavior by giving in.

❖ **Head off a tantrum by offering choices.** For example, tell the student she can either play with the green pony or the yellow pony in the doll center. You have chosen the center, but she gets to choose what to play with.

❖ **Explain that there are different rules for home and school.** Crying for something may work at home, but it does not work at school.

❖ **Establish a classroom "thinking chair" apart from the time-out area.** Send a student to the thinking chair to calm down. Unlike time-out, explain that he may get up when he is ready to rejoin the class.

Sensitive and Empathetic Children

❖ **It is important to discuss, acknowledge and accept students' feelings.** No one is happy all of the time. Take time to listen to sad students and comfort them as best you can.

❖ **Plan for how to present sensitive subject matter and consider how students will react.** Some students may gloss over the spider's fate in *Charlotte's Web* or not mind that the class's pet lizard eats live crickets, while others may feel great sadness.

❖ **Explain sad things in a positive way.** For example, state that it would not be pleasant for dinosaurs to be walking around instead of being extinct. They would trample the school, buckle the roads, and eat people.

❖ **Diffuse situations with laughter.** For example, if a student is sad about the school year ending, joke that you love her so much that she can stay until she is taller than you are! (Be careful not to laugh at the student.)

❖ **Older students may find comfort in friends.** Pair students with buddies and let them work together when one student is going through a sad time.

❖ **For a situation such as an illness or a death in the family, let classmates make cards** to send to the student. It can help just to know his friends are thinking about him.

❖ **If you do not know why a student is sad, use the Draw Your Feelings worksheet (page 109)** to find out. If a student will not divulge feelings, she might share them through her drawings.

Students with Sad Events in their Lives

❖ **Help the student talk about his feelings with you or a counselor.** Getting things out in the open always helps.

❖ **Students touched by divorce or trauma need time to grieve.** Be patient as they work through grief.

❖ **Help classmates be sensitive as needed by explaining why their friend is sad** (when appropriate) and offering suggestions for how to act around the grieving student.

❖ **Never belittle a student's feelings.** "Boys don't cry," and "Big kids don't cry," are inappropriate statements.

❖ **Find out about changes in family situations and ask parental advice** for how to help their child cope.

❖ **During discussions with parents, make sure they know what the student is saying at school.** For example, a student may be sad about parents arguing at home, while they have no idea she is overhearing them.

❖ **On the How Do You Feel Better worksheet (page 110), students can list ideas for how they can feel better.**

Students Who Cry from Fear at New Situations

❖ **Prepare students for their new class by being warm and friendly at Open House.**

❖ **Encourage parents to take pictures of the classroom and school to look over at home, or to arrange a play date with a classmate.** Seeing familiar places or faces can put the fearful student at ease.

❖ **Getting lost is usually a big fear, so give students several tours of their new classroom or school.** Point out landmarks as you go—especially bathrooms!

❖ **New people can be as scary as new places, so introduce students to each other.** Acquaint one small group at a time, then leave them together to do a new activity so they have a chance to get to know each other.

❖ **Sharing a book about a new situation, such as the first day of school, can be helpful.** Send home a reading list for new students.

Students Who are Fascinated by Death

❖ **When answering students' questions about death, you can get put on the spot pretty easily, and it is hard to be prepared.** It is usually safest to give an honest answer when the answer is straightforward, and resort to, "Ask your parents," when the answer is more complicated or has religious implications.

❖ **If a student frequently mentions death, talk with parents about what may have triggered this interest,** and work on a plan to deal with the sadness or questions that arise, if necessary.

❖ **If a student is afraid of losing a family member, let her bring a picture of that person to school.** Allow her to look at the picture when she needs reassurance.

❖ **There are few ways to truly prepare a student for a trauma or death in the family and the inevitable grief that follows.** Time is the best healer, so give the student the time and patience she needs to heal.

Draw Your Feelings

Student's Name: _____ **Date:** _____

Directions: Write and draw about something that makes you happy.

Then, write about something that makes you sad.

How Do You Feel Better?

Student's Name: _____ **Date:** _____

Directions: Everyone is sad sometimes. When you are sad, what can you do to make yourself feel better? Maybe you can make a silly face in the mirror, or sing a happy song that you love. Draw or write some ideas that you or someone else could do to make you feel better.

Sing a Happy Song

Lying

Lying is one of the most difficult behaviors to address. There are so many degrees of lying, and so many reasons for doing it. There is lying to cover up a misdeed, lying by exaggeration, lying in the "tall tale" fashion, and telling a white lie about something so as not to hurt someone's feelings. And frankly, there are many rewards for doing it well, the greatest of which is not getting into trouble for misbehaving. Plus, students hear others tell little lies all the time, and it is hard to explain such gray rules for lying when students see most things in black and white.

Lying often starts out as outright make-believe. A young student who announces, "I have a thousand pieces of candy in my bag," or "I climbed on top of the school and flew off!" is aware that his audience knows he is "telling a story." Storytelling moves into cover-up as a student learns to answer either, "No, I didn't do it," or "I don't know," when asked who made too much noise in the hallway. Lying by exaggeration soon follows as students start one-upping each other and competing for attention: "I went to the beach last weekend?" "Oh yeah? Well I went to the beach AND the carnival ten times!" And it goes on from there.

Most young students are terrible liars. It is usually easy to see when they are lying, although not always. After you learn the signs of lying, which will be different for each student, you can address individual instances of the problem. Plus, you will be able to tell whether a student is a frequent liar or one who just lets the occasional falsehood slip out.

Indicators of Lying
- ❖ **Makes poor eye contact.**
- ❖ **Looks anxious; students who are telling the truth will look relaxed.**
- ❖ **Squirms or mumbles while telling the lie.**
- ❖ **Obviously exaggerates stories.**
- ❖ **Sounds overly earnest: "I did TOO! Really!"**
- ❖ **Statements sound rehearsed**
- ❖ **Statements contradict each other or are inconsistent, or get embellished with each retelling.**

Tricks and Tips for Addressing Lying

- ❖ **Starting in about first grade, it is not a bad idea to set the tone of honesty in your classroom.** Explain that all students start out with a clean record. When they tell a lie, you have to decide every time after that whether you believe them or not. Tell students that you hope they will be honest with you no matter what.

- ❖ **Do not confuse lying with pretending.** Obvious fantasy storytelling is just that—telling a story. It shows imagination in most cases, not dishonesty.

- ❖ **Deal with a student who is lying in a way that is appropriate to her age.** A four-year-old who is trying out a fib for the first time should be redirected to tell the truth. A seven-year-old who lies about punching a classmate on the playground—when

the classmate has a puffy eye and has pointed the finger at the culprit—has earned a parental phone call or similar punishment.

- ❖ **Make the punishment fit the crime.** Misbehaving is one thing, and lying is something else on top of it. It can help to give the student two sets of consequences. For example, say, "If you broke Maya's crayons, you will have to apologize and let her use yours. If you broke her crayons and continue to lie about it, you will have to apologize, let her use yours, and sit out for 10 minutes of recess today." If you can easily verify who broke Maya's crayons, the student will probably choose to tell the truth, in which case you should still inflict the lesser punishment but praise him for being honest.

- ❖ **If you suspect a student is lying, ask detailed questions.** If the answers come easily and are consistent, the student is likely to be telling the truth.

- ❖ **When you ask a question and the student shows signs of fidgeting or avoiding eye contact,** ask your question again, and say something like, "You seem really uncomfortable. Do you want to change your answer? I will appreciate your honesty."

- ❖ **Be especially watchful when dealing with a student whom you think habitually lies.** Witnessing any incidents that could prompt lying can take the guesswork out of a situation.

- ❖ **When a group of students appear to be lying about something, question each student separately,** and ask another adult to keep the rest of the group apart. You can see whether their stories match up without giving them a chance to get on the same page.

- ❖ **Some students use excuses to get out of trouble:** "I could not do my homework because my sister's dance recital lasted until midnight!" "I did not knock over Betsy's tower on purpose. Janal pushed me into it!" If you notice a student consistently making excuses about one particular thing, such as homework or confrontations with another student, talk to the student about it, and focus on the homework or the confrontations, which are probably the deeper problem.

- ❖ **Try to be sensitive to some types of lying.** Students get embarrassed in front of each other very easily, especially as they become old enough to compare themselves to others, and some situations make lying understandable. A student who steals food from friends' lunch boxes and then lies about it does not necessarily deserve a lecture. Instead, find out whether the student is not being fed at home.

- ❖ **When older students lie by telling fantastic stories or greatly exaggerating,** it can mean they feel inadequate in some way. For example, a student who fabricates a story about going on a cruise for vacation may feel bad because she is one of the few who stayed home over spring break. Acknowledge the lie, but think of some ways to put the student in the spotlight. For example, let her read a story she wrote to the class, or post her artwork and praise it. Getting recognition for something real can remove the incentive to lie.

- ❖ **Always confront students about lying in private.** Also, be careful what wording you use. The word *liar* is highly charged, so tread carefully—it is much less inflammatory to ask a student whether she is telling the truth than asking whether or not she is lying.

- ❖ **Do not create "truth traps" for students.** If you know for certain that a student misbehaved, do not bother asking whether he did it. This simply adds fuel to the fire by giving the student an opportunity to lie about a misdeed and get into even more trouble.

- ❖ **If you teach a chronic liar, turn to the student's parents.** Document some examples of lying to share with them, then talk about whether lying is a problem at home. Partner with parents so you can verify stories and implement consistent punishments.

- ❖ **Get students to think about a real-life circumstance where they might be tempted to lie.** Read the stories on the Should I Tell a Lie? worksheet (page 113). Have a class discussion about what they would do in each student's place.

- ❖ **Most students can think of times when they were glad they told the truth, even if it wasn't easy.** On the Telling the Truth worksheet (page 114), let older students write about a time when they told the truth with no regrets later. Ask younger students the questions on the page, and let them dictate their stories as you record them.

Should I Tell a Lie?

Student's Name: _____ **Date:** _____

Directions: Read or listen to the story. Write or tell about how you think the story should end.

Will, Natalie, and Casey were playing on the playground. Their teacher, Mrs. Wilson had asked them not to kick the ball close to the fence. They were kicking the ball and getting closer and closer to the fence, then suddenly it went over. The ball rolled down the street, down a hill, and out of sight. A few minutes later, Mrs. Wilson walked over and asked, "Will, where is the ball?" Will said, "We stopped playing ball. We were tired of it. Mrs. Wilson said, "Casey, what happened to the ball?"

What do you think Casey should say?

_____

_____

Nina and her sister Callie walk home after school. As they were walking, Nina told her sister, "Jordan asked me to come over and play today. I do not really like Jordan, so I told him I had a piano lesson today."

"But your piano lessons are on Mondays. Today is Wednesday," said Callie.

"I know," said Nina, "But I didn't want to hurt his feelings," said Nina.

"But you told a lie, Nina," said Callie. Just then, they heard someone calling Nina. It was Jordan.

"Hey, Nina! I thought you said you had piano lessons today," called Jordan. He turned to Callie. "Does she have lessons on Mondays?"

What should Callie say?

_____

_____

Telling the Truth

Student's Name: _____ **Date:** _____

Directions: Sometimes it is hard to tell the truth. Maybe you did something wrong and you do not want to admit it. Maybe you are afraid to get in trouble. But telling the truth is the right thing to do. Write or tell about a time when you were glad you told the truth, even though it was scary or difficult.

Telling the Truth

Student's Name: _____ **Date:** _____

Directions: Sometimes it is hard to tell the truth. Maybe you did something wrong and you do not want to admit it. Maybe you are afraid to get in trouble. But telling the truth is the right thing to do. Write or tell about a time when you were glad you told the truth, even though it was scary or difficult.

Inability to Build Friendships

So far, this chapter has explored many of the reasons students fail to make friendships. Students who cannot talk easily to friends or who cannot stop talking, who are too shy or angry to connect, who scare away classmates by being too rough, who cry all the time, who are bullies, or who tell lies are hard to befriend. And certainly, correcting these problems will clear the way for students to make friends.

However, there are other reasons that some students fail to form friendships. Some students truly prefer to play alone. Other students end up in classes with students who are just different from them. Consider the situation of a boy who loves to read and play board games who ends up in a classroom full of rowdy, rough-and-tumble boys who race and play football every day on the playground. These students may eventually discover common interests or learn to give and take, but it could be rough going for a while.

Of course, most teachers have plenty to worry about as far as teaching their students without spending valuable classroom time trying to find friends for all of them. But, it does make a difference. Most teachers remember especially good groups who supported and encouraged each other. No one likes to spend an entire year in a classroom that does not seem to "click." So, here are a few extra ideas to help the environment in your classroom evolve into a community

Indicators of Inability to Build Friendships
- ❖ **Plays alone in most situations, or parallel plays long after that behavior usually turns into group play.**
- ❖ **Does not initiate play with others.**
- ❖ **Does not contribute to play. (In a pretend scenario, goes along with what others are doing but does not really play a role.)**
- ❖ **Does not greet classmates upon arrival to school or say goodbye when she leaves.**
- ❖ **Does not have play dates with classmates.**

Tricks and Tips for Helping a Student Build Friendships

- ❖ **Remember to consider the personality of a student before labeling him as lonely or sad.** Some students are naturally introverted and prefer to be alone, and may find it too uncomfortable to play with others at first. Be patient and watch for signs of friendship development.

- ❖ **If you have a few students who seem isolated, study your classroom dynamics.** Seat students who already know each other and are friends in different areas of the classroom.

- ❖ **Consider seating two students who seem a little left out together.** If either of them is looking for a friend, they might find it in the other classmate.

- ❖ **If a student has grown up around plenty of playmates, he has probably already learned to seek out friends** and connect with them. Students with a lot of siblings or with no siblings or nearby neighborhood children may just be inexperienced at making friends. Make friendship a writing assignment or a class discussion. Talk about what it feels like to have a friend, and let students contribute ideas. Then, give each student a copy of the My Pretend Friend worksheet (page 117) to fill out. If students are not yet writing, let them dictate the answers as you write them down.

- ❖ **If your school permits it, compile a class list of student names, addresses, and phone numbers to send home.** This will help parents contact each other about getting their children together.

- ❖ **When the parents know each other they will feel more comfortable about arranging play time outside of class.** Have a class party or "Come Meet My Friends" event early in the year. Invite parents in to see a program, a class project, or for a small party.

- **Not just classmates can form friendships.** Try to overlap your playground time with at least one other class in the same grade level so that students in different classrooms can meet each other.

- **If a new student comes to class and established play groups (or cliques) are already formed, assign a confident classmate to be the new student's buddy.** Ask the classmate to introduce her to others, show her where things are in the school, and explain routines. Giving a classmate the official job of paving the way for the new student may make the transition smoother.

- **Making new friends can seem like hard work, since everyone has to go through all of the getting-to-know-you motions.** Plan some activities with students that do some of the work for them. For example, when you have a new student or a group of students who do not know each other, stand in a circle and let each student say his name and tell something about himself. In a younger classroom, during circle time, let each student stand up and say her name, then lead the class in clapping for that student, saying, "Yay, it's Claudia!"

- **Most preschools do an actual getting-to-know-you unit at the beginning of the year.** However, this can be worth your while in elementary school, too. You can start or culminate the unit with a bulletin board based around kindness. Snap a photo of each student. Post the photos on the bulletin board. Assign students to "graffiti" the board by writing kind comments about each other on it. Tell them that each student should have five comments, to make sure all students get the same amount.

- **Another get-to-know-you graphing activity involves showing students how alike they are.** Send home the All About Me questionnaire (page 118) and ask students and parents to fill it out for homework. When you have the completed questionnaires, graph the results from one answer each day. Students will find out that many of them share preferences and characteristics.

- **Give each student a copy of the Body Cutout (page 118).** Ask parents to donate magazines. (Steer away from magazines with inappropriate content, and remember that women's magazines can contain some pretty graphic health information!) Let each student cut out the body shape and glue on magazine pictures of things she likes. Post the cutouts. Then, let each student walk around the shapes with a note pad and write down the names of at least three classmates who liked one of the same things as she did. She should also record the pictures they have in common.

- **Especially as students get older, teachers tend to focus on academics during parent conferences.** Parents will want to know how their children are doing socially, though—especially parents of kindergartners whose children have just made the leap to "big school." Include this information in your conference. Name the student's friends and share an anecdote or two about classroom interaction. If a student does not have many friends, you can gently offer suggestions for the parent to help her child interact better. For example, you can suggest inviting someone for a play date, or suggest that the parent send her student in with a different lunch box, since classmates tease her third-grade son about his lunch box that is covered in lambs and bunnies. Give this advice gently and tactfully, since students' clothing and other choices often reflect their parents' tastes

My Pretend Friend

Student's Name: _____ **Date:** _____

Directions: Pretend you are going to make a new friend. What kind of friend would you like? Answer the questions to find out what is important to you in a friend.

1. **Circle the answer that you like best.**

   I like a friend who laughs a lot.   I would rather have a friend who is quiet.

2. **Circle the answer that you like best.**

   I want my friend to like what I like.   I want a friend who likes different things.

3. **Circle all the answers you like. I want a friend who:**

   reads a lot   plays sports   likes animals   likes to build things

   likes math   runs fast   loves music   can dance

   rides horses   can draw well

5. **Which is more important in a friend? Circle one.**

   Can keep a secret   Is happy a lot   Does not hurt my feelings or tease me

   Listens to me   Lives nearby   Goes to my school

6. **To be a good friend, the most important thing I can do is** _____

   because _____

   _____

All About Me

Student's Name: _____ **Date:** _____

Directions: Answer these questions to help your classmates learn all about you!

1. How many brothers and sisters do you have? brothers: _____ sisters: _____
2. Are you an only child? The oldest child? The youngest child? In the middle?_____
3. Do you have a pet? _____
4. What color are your eyes? _____
5. What color is your hair? _____

Body Cutout

Cut out the body shape. Write your name on the back. Cut out magazine pictures of things you like. Glue the pictures to the front of your body shape.

Abuse-Responsive Behaviors

All teachers dread the day when they discover that a student is living in an abusive or neglectful household. Even though most schools and daycares have protocol in place for dealing with these situations, there are always gray areas. Teachers ask themselves, "Did I do the right thing? Is this what is really going on? Is it really abuse? Should I really report it or will that cause more harm than good?"

Unfortunately, the sad truth is that although teachers are certainly in a position to make things better, there is a limit to how much you can help because you cannot control the situation at home. However, there are certainly steps you can take to make sure that the student has the best possible atmosphere in the classroom, and that the proper authorities are aware of your observations.

Indicators of Abuse

❖ Signs of **physical abuse** include flinching or cowering (especially at sudden movements), frequent injuries, vague (or overly elaborate) explanations for those injuries, "pattern" injuries (cigarette burns, belt marks, etc.), wearing long sleeves or pants in hot weather to hide injuries, fear of going home, fear of being picked up at school by a particular family member, and withdrawn behavior.

❖ Signs of **emotional abuse** include inappropriate anger and harsh language, extremes in behavior (aggression or submission), disinterest in the parent or caregiver (is indifferent when Mommy arrives to pick him up).

❖ Signs of **sexual abuse** include a drastic change in behavior (such as becoming extremely withdrawn or secretive or fearful), discomfort sitting or walking, urinary tract infections in girls, trouble with toileting issues, inappropriate sexual knowledge or behavior for the age group, fear of a caregiver, shame, heightened interest in her own or others' bodies, and inappropriate sexual language.

❖ Signs of **neglect** include inappropriate clothing (clothing that is wrong for the season, torn and dirty, ill-fitting, or rarely changed); inadequate or missing lunches; coming to school hungry; stealing food; inadequate medical care for illnesses, injuries, or vaccinations; poor hygiene; frequent tardies or absences; seeming unusually self-sufficient; and acting as a caregiver for younger siblings.

Tricks and Tips for Addressing Trauma and Abuse-Responsive Behaviors

❖ **For all possible abuse situations, the cardinal rule is documentation.** Even if you have a very strong "gut feeling" that a student in your class is being abused, intuition will not allow your director or principal to launch an investigation. Use the Documentation form (page 121) to record daily observations about the student. Use the Documentation Summary form (page 122) to help you summarize specific, relevant observations. The Documentation Summary helps you build a case for speaking to parents or possibly referring the case to authorities.

❖ **Although you are the student's ally in cases of possible abuse, tread carefully.** When a child is in danger, it is hard not to charge right into the situation and try to rescue her, but abuse is complicated, especially when a parent or caregiver is involved. Regardless of the situation, children love their parents and feel very attached to them. In your probe to get to the bottom of

things, you can easily find yourself criticizing the parent, which is not appropriate and can make the student stop talking. If you suspect abuse, consult your supervisor or the school guidance counselor before you talk to the student. If the student talks to you spontaneously, keep your comments supportive but neutral. Say things like, "Thank you for telling me this," and take the student seriously but try not to appear shocked or appalled since that may shame the student into silence.

❖ **If your classroom has centers, putting a student in the housekeeping center can help you determine what kinds of behavior are common at home.** For example, a student who lashes out at dolls or who behaves inappropriately with them may be experiencing similar behaviors at home. If a student's behavior becomes too disturbing, redirect him to another area of the classroom. Be sure to document anything unusual.

For physical abuse:

❖ **If you suspect abuse or even harsh discipline, avoid talking about troublesome issues with the parent you think is the abuser until the situation is resolved.** Telling a student's father that he is causing trouble in class is unwise if the father is going to hurt the student at home as a result. If you truly need a parent's help, try to choose a family member whom the student seems to trust.

❖ **Use a soft, gentle voice and careful movements around a student who may be abused.**

❖ **If a student is hitting other students, he may be facing that behavior at home—hitting may be normal.** Redirect a student who is hitting, and talk to the student about why he is hitting his friends.

For emotional abuse:

❖ **An emotionally abused student often has low self-esteem.** Build him up by complimenting his good efforts, praise him when he behaves, and frequently choose his work to display in the classroom.

❖ **Choose the student to be a classroom helper.**

❖ **Help the student foster friendships.** Assign the student to partner with a classmate who is a class leader. A friendship with a stable, well-liked classmate can be a very positive influence on a student who constantly questions her self worth.

❖ **Encourage the student to participate in extra-curricular activities within the school.** If your school has a safety patrol, a group of students who raise and lower the school flag, or who partner with younger students for reading, make sure the student who suffers from emotional abuse gets involved.

For neglect:

❖ **Determining whether there is neglect in a home can be tricky since all families have different ideas about how clean, well-dressed, and well-fed their children should be.** Families also have very different ideas about interacting with their children, and about how much children should look after younger siblings. Learn about family practices as you document possible instances of neglect. In general, students should come to school fairly clean with combed hair and brushed teeth, with a nutritious lunch. They should have had breakfast either at home or at school. And, their responsibilities at home should allow for enough time to sleep, play, and complete homework.

❖ **Keep a supply of extra clothing and hygiene tools** (new toothbrushes, trial-sized toothpaste, combs, hair accessories, wipes, soap, deodorant for older children, bandages, antibacterial gel, and lotion) in a drawer of your desk for students to use if they feel the need.

❖ **Also keep a supply of healthy snacks in your classroom.** A student who comes to school without breakfast would really appreciate a granola bar, single serving canned fruit, a baggie of dried cereal, or whole grain crackers, and milk or juice.

❖ **Consider sending home a polite, carefully worded note to parents regarding specific issues.** For example, you could say, "Gina seems very tired at school. Getting enough sleep at night would help her feel ready to work." Or, you could write, "Monte is very cold when he arrives at school. I have seen him wear his warm jacket once in a while. Please make sure he remembers his jacket each day." If you are unsure about how your note will be received, run it by your principal before sending it.

❖ **If hygiene is a problem, use the Healthy Hygiene Checklist from the previous chapter on Lack of Personal Care and Hygiene (page XX)** to document instances where the student appears uncared-for. This checklist will help you decide whether you need to bring in a professional to evaluate the care of the student.

Documentation Form

Use this form to document issues you notice in students that may warrant intervention. Each student needs a separate form.

Student's Name: _____ Teacher's Name: _____

Date	Behavior	Action	Comments

Documentation Summary

Use this form to summarize the comments you have made on the Documentation form (page 121). Include significant observations, any conversations with third parties (parents, director or principal), and next steps to be taken.

Month/Week: _____ Student's Name: _____

Teacher's Name: _____

Summary of Observations

Conversations with Parents (Dates and Outcomes)

Conversations with Director or Principal

Actions to Be Taken

Unresponsive to Consequences

A big lesson students learn early is that there are consequences for their actions, good and bad. If students behave and work hard, the consequences are good grades, success in school, a happy teacher, and possibly other rewards when their sticker charts are full or when they earn a week's worth of "green light" cards. If students are disruptive or disobedient, the consequences can be things like time out, loss of recess time, loss of rewards, and even conversations with parents. It seems like a simple system, but some students make it not so simple. These are the students who do not respond to consequences, or whose responses are such that they make consequences counterproductive.

With some students, everything is a battle, and imposing consequences can be either nearly impossible or can escalate the situation rather than diffuse it. These students can crave attention, even if it is negative. They can become even more angry and out of control, to the point where they are unmanageable. Or, if they are frequently punished, they can even assume the role of the "bad kid" whose job it is to be as difficult as possible.

Other students do not become angry or even act out more. In fact, they do not show much of a reaction at all. Punishment simply gets a shrug, or at most, an eye roll, as they shuffle off to the time out chair for the third time in a day. Their behavior does not change because they do not care if they have to sit in time out, or miss part of recess. These students may have low self-esteem or just be unaffected by losing privileges that they do not care about in the first place.

Whether their reactions to punishment for poor behavior are over the top or nonexistent, these students present one of the greatest challenges in the classroom. How can you possibly modify behavior in students who fight you tooth and nail, or who just do not care what you do to them? Read ahead to find out some ideas.

Indicators of Defiance
* ❖ **Acts out frequently, repeats undesirable behavior.**
* ❖ **Has extreme or violent reactions to consequences, or runs away.**
* ❖ **Sees the teacher and other authority figures as "bad guys."**
* ❖ **Has no reaction at all to consequences.**
* ❖ **Is resigned to being in trouble.**
* ❖ **Seems to be biding time through punishment until bad behavior can continue.**
* ❖ **Has poor impulse control.**
* ❖ **Shows little remorse.**
* ❖ **Shows little progress over time; does not seem to learn from mistakes or consequences.**

Tricks and Tips for Addressing Defiance

* ❖ **If you have exhausted all of your usually successful means to modify behavior in this student, take a step back from the situation.** Clearly, it is time to get creative and see the student and your reactions to her with new eyes, because what you are doing is not working.

* ❖ **The first step for seeing the situation with new eyes is to shut down your anger and frustration.** If you have reached the point where the student is constantly angry or completely ignores you, you have also reached the point of automatic response. The student, whether he knows it or not, has learned to push your buttons. Make a conscious effort to stop being angry, frustrated, and overwhelmed with this student.

- **Taking a step back will allow you to objectively observe behavior. On the Behavior Patterns form (page 125), record every incident.** Maybe the student is fine during math but acts up in reading. Or, maybe he behaves in every other specials class but refuses to participate in music class. Maybe he acts out on Monday mornings. Once you identify patterns you can focus on possible triggers.

- **Resolve not to give in.** The student is testing boundaries, and if those boundaries never budge, the student will get tired of testing them.

- **Examine your expectations of an unresponsive student, and remind yourself that this student is not an adult, but a child.** You ultimately have the power you need to run your classroom. And the student has all of the immaturity of any other child. Try not to be overwhelmed.

- **Sit down with a trusted colleague or two, and brainstorm new ideas for improving the situation, including the ones listed here.** Jot these ideas down. As you try them with the student, list them on the What Have I Tried? form (page 126), along with comments about how each new strategy worked.

- **Find both positive and negative consequences that matter to the student,** like sitting with a favorite friend, getting to choose the games center, or having to attend a conference with her parents. Once you find them, put the consequences in place.

- **Instead of punishing the student for bad behavior, start praising the student for good actions,** or putting stickers on his chart for those actions. When he no longer expects to be called out for only bad behavior, the desire for negative attention can be replaced by a desire for positive attention.

- **Give in to a student's demands, if this unusual approach will work.** For example, if a student who is perfectly capable refuses to do all of her in-class reading, say, "Summer, I think you should just read three pages instead of the five that the rest of the class is doing. Will that be too much for you?" When you cast the student's refusal to do her work in a light that suggests maybe she cannot do what her friends are doing, she may decide to do the work, just to prove that she can. (This is different

from giving in and moving boundaries. Lowering your expectations is a strategy, enacted on your terms.)

- **Take the student aside and talk one-on-one during a time when you will not be interrupted.** Tell the student the truth about how difficult his behavior is making things for you and classmates. Explain that the purpose of your meeting is to solve the problem together. Really examine his point of view by telling how you feel, then saying, "I want to know how you are feeling." Then, let him talk. Sometimes a lot of frustration is coming from not being understood or listened to, and feeling like a partner rather than "just a kid" could diffuse the built-up anger or rouse the student from indifference.

- **Find ways to connect with the student.** Ask him to be a special helper, either with you, your assistant, or with a specials teacher. If a student gets to do some behind-the-scenes work like set up the P. E. obstacle course, or help you hang student artwork, he will have some vested interest in wanting routines to go smoothly, rather than disrupt them himself.

- **Do not forget to involve parents, especially if a student is acting violently.** Regardless of the situation, hurting other students or attacking you is not acceptable or excusable. Make sure parents and the student know what behaviors will get him sent out of the room to the office. If a student and parent are forewarned and the meeting is documented, you will have no argument when it is time to send the student from the room. And remember, the time to bring parents into the situation is at the beginning of the power struggle, and not when you are at the end of your rope.

Behavior Patterns

Write down incidents with a particularly defiant or disruptive student. Record date, time, what was going on at the time, and the incident. After a couple of weeks of observations, you may spot a pattern that will be helpful in improving the situation.

Student's Name: _____

Date	Time	Place	What Was Going On	Incident	Notes

What Have I Tried? Document the difficult behavior and look for patterns in timing and situations.

Student's Name: _____

Date, Time, Place	Incident	Action Tried	Results

Appendix: Book List

HEALTH AND SAFTEY

Allie the Allergic Elephant by Nichole S. Smith (Jungle Communications Inc., 2002)
Always Be Safe by Kathy Schulz (Children's Press, 2003)
Bear Feels Sick by Karma Wilson (Scholastic Inc., 2007)
The Busy Body Book by Lizzy Rockwell (Scholastic Inc., 2004)
Going to the Dentist by Anne Civardi (Usborne Publishing, 1992)
How Do Dinosaurs Get Well Soon? by Jane Yolen and Mark Teague (Scholastic Inc., 2003)
No Nuts For Me by Aaron Zevy (Tumbleweed Press, 1996)
Please Play Safe by Margery Cuyler (Scholastic Inc., 2006)
Trevor's Wiggly-Wobbly Tooth by Lester L. Laminack (Peachtree Publishers, 1998)
What Makes You Ill? by Mike Unwin and Kate Woodward (Usborne Publishing, 1993)

PHYSICAL DISABILITIES

Arthur's Eyes by Marc Brown (Little, Brown and Company, 1979)
I Can Talk with My Hands (Creative Teaching Press, 1998)
Mama Zooms by Jane Cowen-Fletcher (Scholastic Inc., 1993)

FINGER PLAYS, RHYMING AND WORD PLAY

Big Brown Bear by David McPhail (Harcourt Brace & Company, 1998)
Books by Dr. Seuss
Brown Bear, Brown Bear, What Do You See? by Bill Martin Jr. (Henry Holt and Company, 2004)
Chicka Chicka Boom Boom by Bill Martin Jr. and John Archambault (Scholastic Inc., 1989)
Chicka Chicka 1 2 3 by Bill Martin and Michael Sampson (Scholastic Inc., 2004)
Dinosaur Roar! by Paul and Henrietta Strickland (Dutton Children's Books, 1994)
The Eentsy, Weentsy Spider: Finger Plays and Action Rhymes by Joanna Cole (Troll Associates, 1991)
The Hiccupotamus Hic by Aaron Zenz (Dogs in Hats Children's Publishing, 2005)
In the Small, Small Pond by Denise Fleming (Henry Holt and Company, 1993)
It's Raining, It's Pouring by Kin Eagle (Charlesbridge Publishing, 1994)
Mary Had a Little Jam and Other Silly Rhymes by Bruce Lansky (Scholastic Inc., 2003)
Mrs. Wishy-Washy's Farm by Joy Cowley (Philomel Books, 2003)
Quick as a Cricket by Audrey Wood (Child's Play, 1992)
Ten Little Bears by Kathleen Hague (Scholastic Inc., 1996)
There Was an Old Lady Who Swallowed a Fly by Simms Taback (Scholastic Inc., 1997)
There Was an Old Lady Who Swallowed a Pie by Alison Jackson (Dalton Children's Books, 1997)

FRIENDSHIP

Bear's New Friends by Karma Wilson (Scholastic Inc., 2006)
Best Friends by Sandi Hill (Creative Teaching Press, 1998)
A Book of Friends by Dave Ross (HarperCollins, 1999)
How To Be A Friend by Laurie Krasny Brown and Marc Brown (Little, Brown and Company, 1998)
Just My Friend and Me by Mercer Mayer (Golden Books Publishing, 1988)
The Loudest Lion by Paul Bright (Little Tiger Press, 2003)
Just Be Nice…and Not Too Rough! by Eleanor Fremont (Golden Books, 1998)
Just Be Nice…and Say You're Sorry! by Catherine McCafferty (Golden Books, 1998)

MANNERS

Are You Quite Polite? by Alan Katz and David Catrow (Scholastic Inc., 2006)
Barney Says, "Please and Thank You" by Stephen White (Lyrick Publishing, 1994)
D.W.'s Guide to Perfect Manners by Marc Brown (Little Brown and Company, 2006)
Show and Yell, A Book About Manners by Richard Chevat (Grolier Direct Marketing, 1992)
Time to Say "Please" by Mo Willems (Hyperion Books for Children, 2005)

EMOTIONS

Alexander and the Terrible, Horrible, No Good, Very Bad Day by Judith Viorst (Connecticut Printers, 1972)
Goldie Is Mad by Margie Palatini (Hyperion Books for Children, 2001)
The Grumpy Morning by Pamela Duncan Edwards (Hyperion Books for Children, 1998)
It Happens to Everyone by Bernice Myers (William Morrow and Company, 1990)
L Is for Loving by Ken Wilson-Max (Hyperion Books for Children, 1999)
When Sophie Gets Angry—Really, Really Angry by Molly Bang (Blue Sky Press, 1999)
The Very Cranky Bear by Nick Bland (Scholastic Press, 2008)
The Way I Feel by Janan Cain (Parenting Press, Inc., 2000)
Wemberly Worried by Kevin Henkes (Greenwillow Books, 2000)

CONFLICT RESOLUTION

Hands Are Not For Hitting by Martine Agassi (Free Spirit Publishing, Inc., 2009)
It's Just a Game by John Farrell (Boyds Mills Press, 1999)
Oh, Brother! Someone's Fighting by Nikki Grimes (Golden Books Publishing)
Playground Problem Solvers by Sandi Hill (Creative Teaching Press, 1998)

BEING YOURSELF

The Best Me I Can Be Series (8 books) by David Parker (Scholastic Inc., 2004)
Character Education Series (12 books) by Regina Burch (Creative Teaching Press, 2002)
A Color of His Own by Leo Lionni (Alfred A. Knopf, 1975)
Hooray for You! by Marianne Richmond (Scholastic Inc., 2001)

CONFIDENCE/RESPONSIBILITY/CONSEQUENCES

Arthur's Pet Business by Marc Brown (Little, Brown and Company, 1990)
One Monkey Too Many by Jackie French Koller (Harcourt Brace and Company, 1999)
Ruby the Copycat by Peggy Rathmann (Scholastic Inc., 1991)
Where the Wild Things Are by Maurice Sendak (Harper and Row, 1963)
Yes We Can by Sam McBratney (HarperCollins Children's Books, 2006)

FAMILIES

Bear Hugs by Alyssa Satin Capucilli (Golden Books Publishing, 2000)
Fine As We Are by Algy Craig Hall (Boxer Books Ltd, 2008)
A Hug Goes Around by Laura Krauss Melmed (Harper Children's Inc., 2002)
Just Me and My Mom by Mercer Mayer (Golden Books, 1990)
The Mixed-Up Morning by Mercer Mayer (McGraw-Hill Children's Publishing, 2002)
Something Special for Me by Vera B. Williams (William Morrow and Company, 1983)
You and Me, Little Bear by Martin Waddell (Candlewick Press, 1996)